Days to REMEMBER

ROB COLLISTER

Days to REMEMBER

Adventures and reflections of a mountain guide

Foreword by
STEPHEN VENABLES

bâton wicks

Bâton Wicks, Sheffield
www.v-publishing.co.uk/batonwicks

Netti Collister and Medi in the Nant Ffrancon.

For Netti, with love

First published in 2016 by Bâton Wicks.

 BÂTON WICKS

Crescent House, 228 Psalter Lane, Sheffield S11 8UT UK.
www.v-publishing.co.uk/batonwicks

This book is a work of non-fiction based on the life, experiences and recollections of Rob Collister.
In some limited cases the names of people, places, dates and sequences or the detail of events have been
changed solely to protect the privacy of others. The author has stated to the publishers that, except in
such minor respects not affecting the substantial accuracy of the work, the contents of the book are true.

A CIP catalogue record for this book is available from the British Library.

ISBN: 978-1-898573-76-0 (Paperback)
ISBN: 978-1-898573-77-7 (Ebook)

Design and production by Jane Beagley.
Vertebrate Publishing
www.v-publishing.co.uk

Bâton Wicks is committed to printing on paper from sustainable sources.

Printed and bound by Pulsio, Bulgaria.

Contents

Foreword

Once upon a time, in the early 1970s, when I was young and newly intoxicated by mountaineering, but living far from the mountains, I fed my addiction by reading. I devoured the classic narratives of Eric Shipton, Gwen Moffat, Dorothy Pilley, Hermann Buhl, Lionel Terray and dozens of other mountain heroes. But for contemporary inspiration I relied on the bi-monthly magazine *Mountain*, whose editor, Ken Wilson, had a knack of winkling out those climbers who were doing both interesting stuff and knew how to write about it. To my mind one of the most eloquent of those mountain writers was Rob Collister.

Here was a man who seemed to achieve all the things I aspired to. He had travelled by dog sled to remote peaks in Antarctica. He had climbed some of the hardest ice routes on Ben Nevis and was one of the few British mountaineers then braving winter climbing in the Alps. Long before it became a glitzy media event, he had, in a single day, skied the famous Glacier Patrol from Zermatt to Verbier. In Asia he was setting new benchmarks for ultra-lightweight first ascents of stunning peaks in Chitral, Hunza, Kulu, Kishtwar ... names redolent with the promise of exotic adventure.

One of the most notable of those vintage *Mountain* articles by Rob was an account of the North-West Face of the Gletscherhorn in the Bernese Alps. No Britons had previously attempted this huge ice face lurking behind the Jungfrau in the wild cirque of the Rottal Glacier. In fact it had probably had few ascents *at all* since it was first climbed in the thirties. So, in purely competitive terms – and don't let *any* climber fool you that he or she does not have at least a streak of competitiveness – this was a nice tick to add to the CV. But what comes across in Rob's account – republished here – is not chest-thumping triumphalism, but a sense of delight. Here is someone genuinely loving what he is doing, relishing the difficulties, enjoying the companionship, attuned to every detail of the landscape.

Forty years on, the delight is still there, particularly in his adopted home of Snowdonia. Few people have run, biked and climbed over the mountains of North Wales as assiduously as Rob, and few have observed the landscape so acutely. And few are as knowledgable about its plants and birds. Reading some of his evocative pieces on *Eryri* reminds me just how special that landscape is, particularly in rare cold winters when snow and ice work their transformative magic. The stories also remind me that you don't have to fly thousands of miles to find enchantment – it is right here, on our doorstep. Nor do you have to be climbing some desperate new route at extreme altitude to achieve fulfilment – Rob's account of soloing that classic rock climb *Amphitheatre Buttress* in the Carneddau sparkles with the sheer joy of moving through a vertical landscape.

On a more serious note, when we fly round the world in search of ever more exotic adventures, we burn vast quantities of fossil fuels. Mountaineers contribute their fair share to global environmental degradation. Rob has always been aware of – and has written about – the contradictions inherent in a career that involves taking people into the wilderness, even if he does espouse Schumacher's 'small is beautiful' principle, sometimes to the point of extreme spartanism. (A mutual friend once described the depressingly meagre rations served up by Rob each evening, after yet another gruelling day's march through the Karakoram). Austerity aside, he is the thinking person's climber, as summarised once by his then boss at the National Mountaineering Centre, John Barry, who described him as 'a man of culture, a man of peace, a Renaissance man, all the good bits from *Chariots of Fire*, arrow alpinist, and as fit as a butcher's dog – a deliberately inappropriate metaphor for a conscientious vegetarian.' That pen portrait appeared in an account of the epic first ascent of the East Ridge of Mount Deborah, in Alaska – perhaps the hardest and most committing climb in Rob's long mountaineering career. Of course Barry is gently poking fun, because that is his style, but the mockery is suffused with obvious affection and admiration for one of Britain's great all-round mountaineers. Rob is also a distinguished mountain guide and a fine writer about his chosen way of life. Enjoy these thoughtful, provocative, entertaining evocations of that life.

Stephen Venables

I
Home Ground: WALES

Craig yr Ysfa. The Amphitheatre is the broad gully on the right-hand side.   *Photo: John Farrar.*

1

In my Backyard

Even in the midst of yet another summer when low-pressure systems seemed to queue up in the Atlantic like jumbo jets at Heathrow, there were isolated days of such perfection that it was easy to forgive and forget the rest of the time. Cycling the shady lanes of the lower Conwy valley on a fine June morning when the air felt pleasantly cool on bare legs and the hedgerows were full of honeysuckle and strident wrens, I was reminded why I have chosen to live most of my adult life in Snowdonia. The car was off the road for its MOT and this was clearly a day to be in the mountains. Making a virtue of necessity, I was making my way through Rowen and Llanbedr-y-Cennin up into Cwm Eigiau. From Llanbedr the Ordnance Survey indicates in bold green dots that the track is a byway open to all traffic but it is clearly not much used. Bracken, cow parsley and nettles clogged my chain and forced me off the bike for fifty metres or so until a sunless tunnel formed by hazel coppice subdued the vegetation and made for easier, if muddier, going. The path, brightly edged now with foxglove, campion, herb robert and vibrant blue veronica, narrowed and dropped steeply down to the Afon Dulyn.

The bouldery riverbed was overhung by oak and ash and felt almost tropical in the green luxuriance with which bark and rock alike were smothered by lichen, moss and fern. I carried the bike across a neat unobtrusive footbridge and up on to an unremittingly steep, twisting council road calling for bottom gear and maximum effort. Gradually the angle eased and, as the high tops of the Carneddau hove into view, the road emerged from birch woodland on to a moor of tussock grass and rush and a few sheep.

With easier cycling and gates to open and shut there was much to see and hear that would have been missed in a car. Simple things like the crimson breast and lovely rufous-brown back of a linnet perched on a gorse bush, the descending cadence of a meadow pipit's flight song as it parachuted down to earth, the strange fishing-reel call of a grasshopper warbler, were all familiar enough but at that moment they were a source of wonder and delight. As I pedalled on towards the mountains I was grinning to myself.

At the road's end where cars were parked, it was a simple matter to lift the bike over the locked gate and continue along a wet track to the dam wall, never repaired after it ruptured with tragic consequences in 1925. Beyond the wall the track became rougher and rockier and it would have been a struggle to ride without front suspension at least. Even with, it was quite sufficiently challenging for me. Some hillwalkers seem to dislike mountain bikes on principle, yet in a situation like this they represent a valid example of what Fritz Schumacher called 'intermediate technology'. A modern bike is a highly sophisticated machine yet it is unpolluting, an extremely efficient form of transport, and great fun to boot.

At Eigiau Cottage, a small hut belonging to the Rugby Mountaineering Club, the roof was being re-slated. A farmer, quad bike idling, had stopped for a chat. Suddenly, Cwm Eigiau felt almost busy, if not quite like the nineteenth century must have been when the farms were occupied and the quarries active. The grassy track steepened and the riding was made difficult by several washouts. Finally, sweating and beginning to burn at the back of my neck, I reached the old slate quarry, abandoned since 1890, and hid my bike inside one of its roofless dressed-slate buildings.

Overhead reared the dark verticality of Craig yr Ysfa. A steep little path wound up through scree and bilberry to the broad stony gully known as the Amphitheatre. I was detained awhile by the spectacle of a black beetle gamely manoeuvring a twig three times its own length, but soon I was at the foot of a rock ridge forming the left wall of the Amphitheatre, the start of a favourite rock climb. The guidebook describes it as *Amphitheatre Buttress*, 280-metres long, first climbed in 1905 by the Abraham brothers from Keswick and graded Very Difficult, which means that, in climbing terms, it is not very hard. However, it is by no means a scramble and there are several places where the obvious line is not the easiest, so route-finding acumen is called for. Its popularity over the years is evident from the way holds have been rounded and smoothed by the passage of many feet, demanding extra care.

I was carrying only a bum bag containing a windproof and some sandwiches. With no rope, helmet, harness or rock shoes, the preparatory rituals were reduced to cleaning mud from the soles of my trainers. Solo climbing is obviously more hazardous than climbing with a partner and a rope but this route was well within my technical ability and soloing confers a freedom to focus totally on the rock and to be absorbed by the place without the distraction of belays, climbing calls and all the paraphernalia that normally goes with climbing. Feeling a little stiff and awkward at first, I soon started to relax on solid, slabby rock, reassuringly in balance. Gaining height I began to revel in the precise placing of hands and feet and the flow of continuous careful movement. The crux, one hundred metres up, was a steep little rib, its holds polished, the drop down into the Amphitheatre horrifying. More than ever, it was a time to suspend the imagination and focus intently on the few feet of rock immediately ahead. A hand twisted inside a crack provided a perfect jam for a strenuous pull up and a jug-handle hold just where most needed made the moves above feel exciting but secure.

I paused for a moment to savour the situation. Ledges on the far side of the Amphitheatre were a distinctive blue-green flecked with yellow, the fleshy leaves of roseroot and the yellow orbs of globeflower hinting at a different, less acid geology. Overhead, the sky was still a flawless blue. A peregrine ducked silently behind the skyline and did not reappear. A series of short walls and little paths in the heather led to a pinnacle, or gendarme, four-metres high. On the far side of this feature the ridge narrowed to the proverbial knife-edge. George and Ashley Abraham were professional photographers who made a habit of taking a huge plate camera and tripod with them whenever they went climbing. A photograph in their book *Climbing in North Wales* (1911) shows a climber sitting uncomfortably astride this ridge, nudging forward with difficulty. One hundred years later, it seemed simpler to swing across the slightly overhanging left wall on enormous handholds.

Above, the ridge steepened again to a final bastion. Interesting climbing all at once became too hard for comfort and I was forced to beat a retreat and find an easier way. Finally, a line of holds led leftwards across a gully wall and then abruptly the ground was horizontal, the climb over. In front, on the far side of Nant y Benglog, the Ogwen valley, were the hazy grey shapes of the Glyderau and the familiar dark shark's fin of Tryfan. Far below, specks of colour and faint shouting indicated another party embarking on the climb, but the top of Craig yr Ysfa was deserted. Eating my lunch overlooking the Amphitheatre, it seemed quite likely that the Abrahams and their friends would have sat in the same spot all those years ago and I wondered if their provisions were as substantial as their camera.

The summit of Carnedd Llewelyn beckoned and it was much too fine a day to ignore the summons. After the care-filled concentration of the climb, the walk up was a blissfully untaxing stroll. Others were picnicking at the cairn, so with a nod and a smile I crossed the summit plateau, a confusing, disorienting place in mist or storm, and descended a boulder field towards Foel Grach. Just past the little outcrop known as Tristan's Cairn I cut right to reach a branch of the Afon Eigiau, passing chunks of metal debris from a crashed aircraft and the bloated, buzzing carcass of an unfortunate sheep that had ventured too far on to a patch of bright green floating sphagnum. In no time I was back at the bike and clattering down to the dam. Another wet potholed track led to Coedty reservoir above Dolgarrog through damp woods of willow and alder, filled with the repetitive call of the chiffchaff and the limpid song of its almost identical cousin, the willow warbler. My way home took me past the Dutch Pancake House near Rowen which, to anyone tired, hungry and exceedingly thirsty, is to be thoroughly recommended.

Back home, browsing through a journal of the John Muir Trust over yet another cup of tea, I came across a reference to 'the spiritual qualities for which humans value wild land: freedom, tranquillity and solitude'. It struck me that I had experienced all three for much of that day in Cwm Eigiau.

Ysgolion Duon (the Black Ladders) seen from Yr Elen.

2

A Winter's Day

I am no sceptic when it comes to climate change, but there were occasions during the longest, coldest winter since the seventies when I had to remind myself that weather and climate are not synonymous. In Snowdonia, driving was often hazardous and parking difficult as councils did not see fit to clear car parks of snow. Nevertheless, huge numbers of people persisted and made it into the mountains to enjoy the winter conditions.

Snowdon was thronged, as ever, with hosts of poorly equipped walkers skittering precariously upwards on paths made icy by the passage of many feet. Cwm Idwal was packed with better-equipped climbers kicking and hacking their way up falls of vertical ice. I visited both at different times and enjoyed mountain days that were exhilarating and companionable. Yet there is an awareness of sights and sounds, sensations and feelings that is easily neglected in the cheerful chatter of a day out with friends.

The most memorable day of the winter, for me, was midweek in February when I set off into the Carneddau alone.

It seemed an auspicious start when I was able to park without difficulty in Gerlan above Bethesda. I knew for certain it was going to be a good day when three builders, cradling mugs of steaming tea in cold hands, gave me an affable good morning as I passed. The sun shone in a rare blue sky, but puddles and seepages were still frozen hard as I made my way up a shaded lane and into the walled fields of the ffridd. There was not a soul about and very few sheep. Soon I was on the open mountain, passing close to the barely discernible walls and crude hut circles of a prehistoric settlement, following the Afon Caseg up towards its source.

Quite unlike Snowdon or the Glyderau in character, the Carneddau are big, spacious hills, protected from crowding by 'the long walk in', where the feet can roam at will and the spirit expand. Cutting the corner of a bend in the valley, not possible dry-shod in summer, I was able to cross the river on a snow bridge. Care was needed as the snow, through repeated cycles of thaw and freeze, was iron hard, too hard for the edge of a boot to gain purchase. It would have been easy to slide off into freezing, fast-flowing water. The valley narrowed and its sides steepened almost to a gorge, creating a sense of passing through a portal into an inner sanctum beyond. High up on the left, a projecting spear of rock on Carreg y Garth Isaf was tipped gold by the sun, as if freshly drawn from the molten core of the world. On the other side, the rocks and scree of Yr Elen were speckled by new snow, like a ptarmigan in summer, though sadly we do not have ptarmigan here in Wales. Recrossing the stream, a final steep pull brought me to Ffynnon Caseg, a secluded little lake ringed by the abrupt mountain walls of Foel Grach, Carnedd Llewelyn and Yr Elen, one of my favourite places in Snowdonia.

I had entered a true winter world now. There was not a blade of grass to be seen and the lake had a thick carapace of ice, though I did not push my luck by walking across it. The flanks of the mountains had been engulfed by snow and the upper rocks, coated in rime ice by a moist wind, were just catching fire in the sun, reminiscent more of Patagonia than Snowdonia. That is the alchemy of winter; it has the power to transform the familiar into something strange, the everyday into the extraordinary. These were no longer friendly grassy hills, they were mountains to be taken seriously. I strapped crampons to my boots and took the ice axe off my pack.

Many years before I had approached Yr Elen on ski from the other side, from Cwm Llafar, and as I approached the summit I had been intrigued to find the footprints of a fox emerging from a steep narrow gully to the north. Peering down it I had resolved to return one day and climb it myself. Years passed. Snow in North Wales became a rarity, and I seemed to be away in higher mountains more and more in wintertime. But finally, here I was on a perfect day, in perfect conditions, about to realise that long-held ambition. Three ravens performing flips and rolls high overhead were my only company. All the usual mountain sounds were stilled. There was no bleating of sheep. No splash or trickle of water. None of the usual sighings and rustlings of wind. Even the jets and helicopters of the RAF seemed to be on holiday. In Leslie Stephen's phrase, 'The pulse of the mountain is beating low'. The crunch of my crampons seemed loud in the stillness and somehow reassuring. There is something slightly unnerving about total silence, as if a veil between self and place has been removed and one must tread warily.

Savouring the moment, conscious that in a small overcrowded country I was privileged to have this place to myself, I cramponed beside the lake and up towards the back wall of the cwm, where my gully was an obvious gash in the summit rocks. As the slope steepened I noticed a line of footprints heading in the same direction. For a moment, I thought they might have been made by a fox again, but they turned out to be bootprints, little pigeon-holes in the snow-ice made by inexperienced climbers kicking at a right angle straight into the slope. Cannier climbers keep their feet flat as much as possible, relieving the strain on calf muscles and tendons and allowing the maximum number of crampon points to bite. As the gully narrowed, however, the slope reared up until I was happy to use the old steps. For a moment or two, attached to the mountainside by no more than a couple of inch-long metal spikes on each boot, I wondered if I should have brought a second axe for security. When the difficulties eased and I emerged from the dark shadowed confines of the gully into the sunlit spaciousness of the ridge, it was with a sense of joyous release to which adrenaline no doubt contributed. I wandered out on to a projecting spur to look back down the way I had come, on the thirty years and more of personal history as well as the tapering funnel of ice. Then I made my way back to the ridge and sat on the summit in shirtsleeves eating my sandwiches. Concerns about economic recession and a foreboding about what climate change might mean for my first grandchild, soon to be born, were momentarily forgotten. For a few brief minutes I was conscious only that I was, in Frederic Harrison's words, 'a marvellous atom in a marvellous world'. On the other side of the Nant Ffrancon, Elidir Fawr was a striking conical silhouette. Nearer at hand, the huge cliffs of Ysgolion Duon, the Black Ladders, dominated Cwm Llafar. To the north, across the Menai Straits, lay the characteristic whaleback of Puffin Island. Each familiar shape was a repository for a host of memories of days, and sometimes nights, gone by. I lingered for at least half an hour relishing the warmth, but also the stillness and the silence, so rare in this noise-filled day and age, so important yet so often undervalued. Reluctantly, I stood to go. I had an arrangement to meet a friend at the indoor climbing wall near Waunfawr and I was going to be late. Truly, from the sublime to the ridiculous.

Maen y Bardd neolithic cromlech on Tal y Fan.

3

Walking through Time

There is a Welsh word 'cynefin' which refers to the territorial instinct of sheep, causing them to become attached, or hefted, to a particular piece of mountain. It is a sense of belonging which, once developed, is passed on from ewe to lamb indefinitely and is still, despite ubiquitous grant-aided fencing, worth a lot to the hill farmer. Sometimes, the term is applied to the feeling the Welsh – some of them anyway – have for their homeland. I am not Welsh, and not allowed to forget it, having failed utterly in forty years to learn the language. I am an incomer, a white settler as a friend once fondly called me. Yet I do have a strong sense of belonging in the mountains of Snowdonia – to the landscape if not to the culture.

I once lived for the best part of a year in New Zealand and though I loved every moment of it, I was never tempted to emigrate, and sometimes even felt a little homesick for the 'green, green hills' of Wales.

11

It was certainly not the weather I missed, nor the midges, nor the crowded roads of summer, or even the walking and climbing. Rather, I found myself thinking nostalgically of unspectacular things like small churches, dry-stone walls encrusted with lichen, derelict sheep folds tucked away in remote hollows and stumbled upon by chance, and those massive, mysterious stones that were carefully embedded in the earth by men rather than dumped at random by retreating ice.

Conwy Castle is a constant reminder, hereabouts, of the interminable bloody wars that kept the Saeson (the English) out of Wales from 1066 until 1282, and of the later uprising led by Owain Glyndwr and the retribution that followed. But one cannot walk far in the hills behind Conwy without coming face to face with evidence that people have lived, farmed and fought here for much longer than that.

From my home at the lower end of the Conwy valley, a thirty-minute walk through attractive mixed woodland and up a steep, wet bridleway between high stonewalls, brings one to an old church. Squat and grey, within a protective wall, it seems organic, as if it has grown out of its craggy surroundings. Undoubtedly, its stone would have been quarried locally, the oak for its roof timbers felled nearby. Between memorial stones, the grass is grazed by sheep rather than mown by a machine. Tucked under Tal y Fan, northern outlier of the Carneddau, the little church seems of the mountains. The interior is simplicity itself – some pews, a stone font, a lectern, a decrepit organ and some faded inscriptions in Welsh on the wall behind the altar. Little else. I am always moved by the bareness, the quietness and a powerful sense that this is a place where worship has been valid for a very long time.

For me, what makes Eryri (Snowdonia) unique is not so much its rugged grandeur, or the sense of space and perspective found on its summits, or the challenge of scaling its ancient rocks, or the poignant fascination of its dwindling arctic-alpine flora – all of which can be found in other mountains – it's the wealth of human history to be found everywhere. Nowhere is this sense of human interaction with the landscape over countless generations more keenly felt than at this old church. Yet it is also a reminder of how depopulated these hills have become. Originally built in the thirteenth century, the church was enlarged in both the fifteenth and sixteenth centuries to cater for an expanding community. Few live up here now. Dotted with ruined farms, this landscape is probably emptier today than it has been for four thousand years. Stone circles, standing stones and sunken trackways bear witness to a prehistoric past when the climate of Britain was warmer and drier, and this would have been a thoroughly desirable region in which to graze animals and grow a few crops. The spring in one corner of the churchyard may well have been a place of healing in those Bronze Age times, as it was in the nineteenth century, or the dwelling of a Celtic deity perhaps. By the sixth or seventh century AD the climate would have been cooler and wetter but when Christian missionaries arrived from Ireland it would have made sense to build their first church close to a site already sacred to local people. It may be coincidence, but only fifty metres from the well is a substantial hut circle. It is obscured by tussock grass now, with only a solitary, ivy-choked thorn tree to provide a clue, but in post-Roman times it would have been no ordinary roundhouse. It does not seem entirely fanciful to imagine that this was the original church.

Today, the church is still in use. Even in winter, there are often freshly cut flowers on the altar. Once a month, from May to September, there is an afternoon Sunday service. It is an informal affair, usually well-attended with walking boots and wellies much in evidence and dogs lying at their mistresses' feet. In good weather, sunlight streams through the open door and, in quiet moments, a blackbird can be heard singing outside. It feels right. In the Celtic church, man was still very much a part of nature. For the rest of the time, the visitors' book reveals that I am not alone in being affected by the sanctity of the empty church, without need of liturgy or ritual. A 'still, small voice of calm' can be heard, too often drowned out in hurried, unmindful lives. Who knows, maybe what we feel is not just the essence of St Celynin's message, but what made the well holy long before that, something mysterious and unknowable, but present for all that.

Be that as it may, a grass trackway skirting the lower slopes of Tal y Fan brings one 'in a kilometre or two' to an even older site, a small hill fort whose shallow ditches and stone ramparts are still clearly defined after two thousand years. It is a wonderful vantage point from which to survey the broad, fertile fault line of the Conwy valley. But the interior, the top of a small knoll, is no more than thirty metres across. Not many families could have squeezed in there and it is unlikely that there would have been room for animals as well. On the other hand, such a small area could have been quite effectively defended by a few determined, or desperate, people.

In pre-Roman days, or in the lawless times after the Romans had left, the danger would usually have been short-lived. The threat was most likely to have been from seaborne raiders, wolves of the sea, marauding up the Conwy, who would not have been interested in sieging a fort and maybe sustaining heavy losses. Like a wolf pack, which cannot afford too many deaths or injuries in a hunt, they would have been quite content to loot a village, carrying off whatever had been left behind. The sudden alarm call, the anxious, panting run uphill to the fort, the despair as columns of smoke rise from the burning thatch of roundhouses on the hillside below, the fearful wait for what might happen next; all seem very remote on a summer's afternoon in the twenty-first century.

Nonetheless, they are imaginable scenes. Much harder to visualise are the ceremonies that must have taken place at a site further downhill, maybe three-thousand years before the fort was built. This is a Neolithic or late Stone Age cromlech, a communal burial chamber created by some-how manoeuvring a huge capstone weighing many tons on top of several carefully positioned rock uprights. Originally, the chamber would have been concealed within a large cairn of earth and stone, no doubt with significant herbs and shrubs planted on or around it. For the builders of this family vault were early farmers, hunters and gatherers still, but settled, with domesticated animals and beginning to grow crops and vegetables.

Although gaunt and skeletal from a distance without its protective mound, there is still something womb-like about the enclosed cavity of this tomb. It is not hard to associate it, as archaeologists do, with a venera-tion for Mother Earth and a belief in death and rebirth as part of a natural cycle (a veneration and a belief that we lost long ago, to our cost, as we are beginning to realise). But what chiefly gives this place its strange power is that it has been left alone. True, the landscape has changed over the millennia. The scrub forest which once would have grown to the summit of Tal y Fan is long gone; the distinctive tracery of stone walls is relatively recent, mostly from enclosure times two hundred years ago; the double row of electricity pylons marching over Bwlch y Ddeufaen (Pass of the Two Stones) is the twentieth century's contribution. But it has been spared the Ministry of Works metal railings and the inevitable interpreta-tion board. Above all, it has been spared the trivialisation that comes with an endless procession of visitors. Although not so very far from a road, it is a wet, muddy walk from any direction, so not much frequented.

As Jacquetta Hawkes once wrote, 'Cafés and chewing gum, car parks and conducted excursions, a sense of the hackneyed induced by postcards, calendars and cheap guidebooks has done more to damage Stonehenge than the plundering of some of its stones ... Man made it and man has destroyed it, the whole action taking place in the realm of the imagination.'

A hundred yards away is another burial site, superficially very similar, with a capstone supported by uprights, but this one is smaller, embedded in the ground and takes some hunting for among the bracken. It is believed to date from the Bronze Age, a thousand years later, when religious practice had changed to individual burial and later, cremation. I remember the shock and a strong sense of the profane with which I discovered a plastic bottle, with its bright red Coca-Cola label, lying on the floor of this chamber, as if placed there deliberately. Elitist it may be, but I pray that this trackway is never surfaced and that these places never become tourist attractions.

From lower down the Roman road, sheep-trods lead across a more wooded hillside through medieval field systems where wild daffodils bloom in the spring and past ruined farms abandoned probably in the 1930s, back to the nineteenth-century lead-miners' cottages where I live. The past is everywhere in this landscape. I think again of Jacquetta Hawkes, musing at the end of her wonderful book A Land on how, 'I see the present moment as a rose or a cup held up on the stem of all that is past'. We are inheritors and to recognise and value the past that is around us is to enrich the present and to care for the future.

Prehistoric settlement above Llanfairfechan.

4

Hidden in the Grass

At 610 metres Tal y Fan, the northernmost outlier of the Carneddau, is a miniature but fascinating mountain. A cursory glance at the map shows a marked contrast between its southern and northern flanks. The south side is characterised by long straight walls dividing the land into neat strips, a hallmark of the Enclosure Acts of two hundred years ago when clerks in London drew lines on the map with scant regard for topography. However, on the north side, there are very few walls, or fences, for this has remained common grazing and is now mostly access land. Apart from the summit and the Roman road running from Rowen to Abergwyngregyn, this is empty country frequented much of the year mainly by wild ponies, choughs and the occasional fell-runner. A closer look at the map reveals that Tal y Fan was an area much favoured by ancient man. Matched only by Ardudwy, further south, a wealth of prehistory is to be found all round the mountain. It is a landscape full of settlements, homesteads, enclosures, forts, house platforms, hut circles, stone circles, standing stones, cairns and more. Many of them, though by no means all, are recorded for our benefit by the Ordnance Survey in archaic script on its 1:25000 sheets.

Among the most intriguing are the sites described as 'burnt mounds'. On the ground these do not leap out at you and there is certainly no trace of burning to be seen. It was years before I discovered that they are in fact mounds of burnt stones, usually no more than a metre high, that have become covered with grass and moss and are easily overlooked. What is distinctive about them is that they form a horseshoe shape quite different to the circular cairns of burial mounds. It is believed that these are places where Bronze Age people four thousand years ago dug out troughs which were then lined with wood or clay. In these troughs water could be brought to the boil by adding hot stones from a fire close by. As they cooled the stones were removed and dumped beside the trough creating a character-istic semicircle around it. Originally, archaeologists believed they were used by hunting parties to cook meat while out in the field. Now, opinion seems to have shifted towards a more social function like the washing of clothes and bodies, or possibly even a form of sweat lodge, as well as cooking. On the upland grassy plateau between Tal y Fan and the coast there are at least eight sites shown on the map, most of them not too far from a settlement, hut circles or other signs of prehistoric habitation. All are close to small streams and there would have been no shortage of firewood. Bronze Age Europe was warmer and drier than any other time since the last ice age and, despite significant clearance by early farmers, scrub forest would still have been growing up to the summit of Tal y Fan. Many of these mounds are on slopes facing west so they would have been pleasant, sunny spots to hang out and, who knows, people then may have appreciated the view across the Menai Straits to Puffin Island and Anglesey just as much as we do. It is easy to imagine these sites as meeting places where small local communities regularly congregated.

Another example of enigmatic artefacts that are by no means easy to find, are what the Ordnance Survey calls 'incised stones'. The words on the map are in ordinary rather than archaic script, implying that the OS believes them to be from historical times, usually taken to mean once events began to be written down for posterity by the Romans. There are a number of such stones in this area where grooves have been cut in the surface or edges of flat rocks possibly by the sharpening of knives or swords. They are also known as 'arrow stones' and a good example is to be found on the north side of the Afon Ddu, which flows from Bwlch y Ddeufaen down into Llanfairfechan. About 150 metres south-east of a large cellular sheepfold is a granite post with the figure 5 inscribed on it. This is a marker for the Llanfairfechan Upland Walk, a highly recommended circular excursion from the village. The arrow stone with its incised grooves is at your feet a mere three metres to the south. Another site is in the triangle of land formed between the Roman Road and the track leading north to Carreg Fawr and Llanfairfechan. In the same vicinity is what the Gwynedd Archaeological Trust calls a 'Roman incised stone', a small boulder with a motif of three squares inside each other. Some believe this to be a board for Nine Men's Morris, a game known to date from Roman times, though it would need cleaning and re-instating to the horizontal to play on it now.

Even more mysterious in terms of both age and function is the so-called 'cup-marked stone' to be found nearby, just inside the mountain wall on well-drained grazing above Cammarnaint Farm. To my untutored eye the mass of little hollows on the surface of a flat slab of rock could easily be natural weathering. With the eye of faith, however, one could imagine them being ground out with stone implements which could put them back in the Stone Age. For what purpose is anyone's guess, though they have been described as prehistoric art. Somewhere not far away is another arrow stone reputed to have more than a hundred incisions, though I have yet to find it.

None of these sites are spectacular in themselves, it has to be admitted, and their meaning is elusive. Yet the hunt for them is absorbing and the setting magnificent, if the dreadful pylons marching over from the Conwy Valley can be ignored. Perhaps it is an illustration of the adage that it is better to travel hopefully than to arrive. Stepping off the beaten track to find them is also a reminder that what we think of as grasslands are in fact a mosaic – ever changing according to aspect and drainage – made up not only of grasses but sedges, rushes, heathers, gorse and bracken, as well, and hidden beneath them are a multitude of different mosses, liverworts, lichens and fungi. Above all, these places are a reminder of how lived-in this landscape has been, however wild and empty it may feel today. In this country we are never explorers, we are inheritors.

Asplenium septentrionale, the forked spleenwort.

5

A Botanical Treasure

One summer's day I found myself walking in the Gwydyr Forest above Betws-y-Coed. Despite the omnipresent Sitka spruce, this is a beguilingly complex area, full of hidden gems – little lakes, ruined farmsteads, stone walls buried in the trees, unexpected clearings in which smallholdings are still being worked – where something of interest nearly always seems to occur. I was taking part in a mammal survey so I was looking out for scats rather than plants. Stepping off a forestry track, however, to investigate the spoil from an old lead mine, my eye was caught by a dark fur growing among the orange-brown tailings at my feet. Bending down for a closer look, I realised that the plant was a mass of narrow, dark green leaves, mostly divided at the end. On the underside, these fronds were covered with dark sori, or spore capsules, confirmation that this was a fern, albeit an uncommon one. I recalled an essay about old mines by

Bill Condry in which he remarked, 'As for plants, though most of them shudder at the poisonous ground near lead mines, there are a few that seem to prefer it. There is that rare little fern, the forked spleenwort, for instance.' Rare it may be, but here it was growing in profusion, thick clumps of it scattered over an area of flat open ground some twenty metres square. Highly susceptible to slugs and snails, it is thought that this may have something to do with its propensity for such toxic habitats.

Although I had not found it on a lead mine before, I first made the acquaintance of this fascinating if unobtrusive plant many years ago. It was growing on a wall in a field near Gwydyr Castle, a site I had been told about, but it still took some hunting to locate and all the while I was expecting to be accosted for trespassing. Once spotted it is very distinctive but it is easy not to notice it in the first place. Much later I came across another essay by Condry about a walk near Llandrillo, in the Berwyns, in which he describes an encounter with the plant. 'I left my car and started up a lane climbing to the south. But then at the roadside I found a botanical treasure, one of those freak ferns beloved by Victorian fern collectors, its fronds ending in a fork instead of tapering to a point.' Sites like these prompted the authors of the *Mountain Flowers* volume in the New Naturalist series to opine that forked spleenwort is a lowland rather than a mountain plant, in Snowdonia at any rate. Yet Dewi Jones, in *Plant-life in Snowdonia*, writes that it was first recorded here by Edward Lhuyd, of Snowdon Lily fame, near the top of Carnedd Llewelyn, and later, in the nineteenth century, by William Wilson near Twll Du, the Devil's Kitchen, while he himself has seen it on Moel Hebog.

My next encounter was certainly in the mountains and quite unexpected. I was standing at the bottom of Clogwyn y Grochan, one of the famous Three Cliffs on the north side of the Llanberis pass. I was belaying a friend who was grappling with the first pitch of a classic HVS rock climb. I had been in the same spot at least twenty minutes, my attention focused on the climber, when my eyes, wandering along the vertical wall beside me, alighted on a patch of dark green sprouting from a crevice a few feet away. I could not think what it might be. Curious, but still with one eye on my partner, I moved across and to my surprise and delight recognised the forked spleenwort. It is infinitely more exciting and satisfying to discover something unusual for oneself, whether by chance or by searching for it, than to be shown it or follow directions. I have to admit that my friend did not share my enthusiasm. Sadly, it cannot be described as a charismatic plant. Ecologically intriguing, yes, but visually appealing it is not.

Although, in Snowdonia forked spleenwort is usually associated with mineralisation, my subsequent sightings were all in rock climbing situations. One was at the bottom of a climb on Craig y Clipiau above Tanygrisiau, again while belaying and with time and opportunity for eyes to rove while the leader was placing protection. Another was on Clogwyn yr Oen in the same locality, halfway up the first pitch of a climb I must have done dozens of times without noticing it. This is less surprising when one remembers that in its demand for total concentration and sustained attention climbing is sometimes likened to meditation. Climbers are minutely aware of every wrinkle and rugosity in front of their noses and a few feet above but of very little else while they are actually climbing. On the other hand it may simply have been a case of familiarity breeding not so much contempt as a form of myopia, a common condition in which one sees only what one expects to see. Either way, these dry bare Moelwyn crags looking south over the vale of Ffestiniog towards Trawsfynydd nuclear power station, are clearly to the liking of this fern, for on one of them, the little-visited Clogwyn Holland, there is even a climb named after it – *Septentrionale*, V Diff, first climbed in 1932 by J. Elfyn Hughes, the guidebook tells me, though I confess that it is still on my 'to do' list.

A continental species, the forked spleenwort, *Asplenium septentrionale*, in Britain is near the northern limit of its geographical range and it has been suggested that this may explain its preference for steep, dark-coloured rock which quickly absorbs warmth from any sun available. This seems to be more important than the acidity of the rock, for while the Moelwyn and Llanberis cliffs are rhyolitic and highly siliceous, it is found on basalt and gabbro, both base-rich rocks, in Scotland.

My experience leads me to suspect that there must be much more of this fern about than is generally appreciated. It just happens to grow not only around lead mines but also in places unlikely to be visited by botanists, or even mere plant-hunters like myself, unless they happen to be climbers and it is easily overlooked even then. The forked spleenwort is undoubtedly the ugly duckling of the Asplenium genus but, beauty is in the eye of the beholder, and sometimes a little mystery and elusiveness can compensate for a lack of more showy charms. It certainly never fails to captivate me when I come across it.

Remains of a Dakota aircraft in a bog below Llyn Edno.

6

Going for a Walk

One morning I woke up early intending to be on my way over the hills by
sunrise. In this I was thwarted for the sky was overcast and although down
the valley in the east the sky crimsoned with effort, the sun was stifled by
cloud before it could clear the horizon. In the dim early morning light,
hawthorns in bloom were creamy watercolour explosions on the grey canvas
of the sheep-walk, conifer plantations a dark frame to the muted picture.

Twenty years have filled this landscape with personal significance.
Memories tumble over each other as I follow the upward twists and turns
of the forest track beside the rushing river. Here is the spot where a much-
loved collie went into convulsions, dying within minutes, probably from
strychnine put out for a fox, while the baby, oblivious, played happily
in a ditch. Across the river is the clearing where, one snowy Christmas
Day, a different dog caught and killed a red squirrel, the last we ever saw

in the valley. This is the bend where a rally car skidded off the track and rolled into the river, and where some acoustical trick causes the water to sound always as if a car is approaching. The steep tunnel-like ride up to the top of the forest is the way I toiled once in deep snow with Nedw Pritchard (a local farmer) looking for some missing horses. Nedw's English was never easy to follow, but I loved to listen to his tales of forestry and farming stretching back fifty years. He is dead now, the house and land sold off separately.

Out on the moor, clear of the sheltering spruce, a strong cold wind blows away nostalgia. Wide views of Arenig, Aran, Cadair Idris and the Rhinogydd jerk me back to my present purpose, which is to follow the watershed of the Moelwynion in a broad arc from Glasgwm, near Pen-machno, to Capel Curig. I head west over the moor, skirting another tree-filled valley, following sheep-trods, which avoid the worst of the rushes and tussock grass. A meadow pipit flies out from under my feet and, stooping, I locate four olive-speckled eggs inches from my boot.

Shortly afterwards, the unmistakable scream of a nesting peregrine snatches my attention aloft to glimpse the familiar silhouette slicing across crags high above. I search unsuccessfully for the nest site with my binoculars and continue on my way. Well past the crags, on the shores of a small dam, some instinct makes me glance back. Flying low and boldly close are two birds, side by side, one larger than the other. Tiercel and falcon, male and female, they are unmistakably shooing me off their territory. I go, gladly and uplifted.

Cresting a rise, the A470 lies not far below, descending from the Crimea Pass to the first quarries of Blaenau Ffestiniog. Two kilometres away on the far side, many millions of pounds are being spent and a small but lovely piece of oak woodland obliterated, in order that motorists may speed faster down one of the finest valleys in Wales. However, it is still early and there is no traffic yet.

Over the road a cry from above has me thinking peregrine again, but the sound is subtly different and the profile, when I see the bird, is sparer, slighter, longer tailed – a kestrel. White mutes dribbling down the front of a slender rock pillar betray the nest site. Nearby, a ring ouzel – our mountain blackbird with a conspicuous white crescent on its chest – is becoming agitated. The nest must be close and when a quick search reveals nothing, I take the hint and move on.

Even in the middle of June the flanks of Allt Fawr are soggy underfoot, a haven for sundew and butterwort. I pass a little dam, one of many scattered about the hills behind Blaenau, built to provide power for the slate quarries and mines. Although the heyday of the slate industry was the nineteenth century, slate is still being extracted from the earth in Blaenau. A siren sounds way below and a few minutes later the charge goes off in Llechwedd quarry, the other side of the road. Just below the summit I pause to study the dust cloud through the binoculars, then examine the system of tips and inclines leading up to the still-active quarry at Bwlch, high on Manod Mawr. Temporarily sheltered from the wind I enjoy the rest, relishing the knowledge that around the shoulder of Allt Fawr, only a few yards away, this noise and dust and activity will be out of sight and out of mind. There, one can stride for miles unimpeded over a landscape of rough grass, rock outcrops and innumerable little lakes, beloved by sandpipers and the occasional greenshank. Snowdonia is no wilderness. Its mountains are rapidly shrinking pockets of relative wildness threatened by over-popularity as much as anything; but still, in certain places at certain times, the spirit can be liberated and take flight. This wide expanse of the Moelwynion has always been such a place for me.

However, when I do contour round the summit rocks to the plateau beyond I am confronted, to my consternation, by a large, new, wooden post. Fifty metres away is another and beyond that another. They are the straining posts for a fence, clearly; the fresh tracks of a quad bike show how they have been carried up. Amazed, I hurry across the plateau to see where the posts lead. I turn aside briefly to examine bogbean in intricate white flower in one of the tiny lakes nestling under Moel Druman, but neither on the ground nor in my mind can I escape those disquieting posts or the accompanying vehicle tracks.

All too soon, the fence becomes a reality – green netting stapled on to flimsy split posts, which will be rotting in ten years and derelict within twenty. More straining posts bend south towards Rhosydd but the completed fence swings north, following the parish boundary. Here, at least, it is following the line of a much older boundary fence whose rusted metal stumps still protrude occasionally. But for what purpose is it being resurrected?

Later, I discover that all over the Moelwyns new fences are going up, some of them electric, and often in places that have never been fenced before. When I try to find out exactly why, the agricultural officer of the national park is less than helpful. The reason, I can only surmise, is that while some farmers are happy to accept government money to stock fewer sheep on their land, allowing it to recover from years of over-grazing, others cannot be bothered, finding it simpler to cram sheep on to their land in order to reap the benefits of a per-capita subsidy. In this absurd situation, sheep are bound to wander to where the grass is greener and there is more of it. Cynefin, an individual ewe's sense of territory which traditionally deters her from straying far, no longer holds good and the only solution, it seems, is to separate different flocks with fences – grant-aided, no doubt.

I walk on along the Moelwyn watershed towards Moel Siabod, angry and confused. A part of me rages against the disappearance of that sense of space and freedom that was the charm of these uplands. I contemplate coming up here at night with a chainsaw and systematically destroying this fence. Perhaps I should lead a monkey-wrench gang of eco-warriors to provide the protection for the land that a spineless national park authority never will. Sometimes I tire of being a sensible, adult member of a democracy when the only values it recognises are profit, convenience and material gain. I remember Swampy, the anti-road protester from Devon, asking reporters from the world's media whether they would have been so interested in him or his cause if he had dutifully written to his MP and waited for something to happen.

Sheep farming in Snowdonia could not exist without the subsidy paid to maintain a 'traditional way of life'. But what is traditional about four-wheel drive roads to the summits, quad bikes that can go almost anywhere, fencing where there was none before and plastic feed-bags blown about by the wind? Yet many hill farmers, or farmers in general come to that, are like belligerent dinosaurs when it comes to the public. A generalisation, of course; but I am still smarting from an encounter the previous week when I was turned back on a right of way near Capel Garmon. I drift into fantasy. Why not take sheep off the land, introduce a few wolves to control the numbers of goats and deer, and let the mountains revert to a natural state? They might not be so easy to walk over but they would become a wonderful habitat for wildlife. And the farmers? The grants and subsidies no longer needed could be used to employ them dismantling fences.

This reverie does not last. After all, farmers like the rest of us, have a living to earn, and I cannot expect them to value what I value. And we mountaineers are no better, really, when it comes to vandalising the mountains for our convenience; even if we do justify it in the name of safety. Look at the marker and abseil poles and the tin shelters littered around Ben Nevis, or the refuge on top of Foel Grach in the Carneddau, or the cairns that bedevil paths everywhere, (like the heads of Cerberus, two more seem to spring up for every one knocked down), not to mention mountain railways, chairlifts, funiculars, fixed anchors et cetera, et cetera. Why do we always bring mountains down to our own size, rather than treating them with respect?

Gloomily, I reflect that all conservation movements, be they to save whales or rhinos, tropical rain forest or ancient woodland, Twyford Down or Newbury, or simply some vestige of wild landscape in Snowdonia, are merely rearguard actions. They are slowing down but cannot halt an inevitable process; they are doomed to ultimate failure in an over-populated world rushing headlong into a materialist abyss. Perhaps cynical resignation is the most appropriate response.

All at once, I become aware of warmth and that the ground around me has been lit by a shaft of sunlight. The cloud is lifting and breaking up. In the west is the distinctive shape of Snowdon and the familiar forms of the Glyderau and Carneddau, to the north looms Moel Siabod and a little below me, enfolded by rock and heather, are the ruffled waters of Llyn Edno. Outlines are sharp, colours clear and fresh.

Equanimity slowly returns, even if acceptance does not. This place will never be quite the same again for me, but I have to recognise that not everyone objects to wire and machines in the mountains, and anyone coming here for the first time might wonder what all the fuss is about. After all, most of Britain is enclosed by fences, and at least there are stiles on this one. But that is precisely why it hurts so much.

At the northern shore of Llyn Edno, I stop to drink from the outflow and recline comfortably against a slab of rock. A raven checks me out, passing overhead slowly, watchfully, without a wing-beat. A pipit emerges from behind a rock with something in its beak, sees me, and flies off in alarm. The wind is sighing among rocks above and bilberry leaves rustle noisily only a few feet away, but this little nook is sheltered and in the warm sunshine my head begins to nod.

I am woken by a faint buzzing. It sounds like a chainsaw but in my drowsy, half-conscious state the notion seems absurd. The buzzing comes again, louder, more insistent, and I remember the fence and the off-cuts strewn about in places. Sure enough, when I peer round the crags at my back, there is a burly figure in a red shirt pouring tea from a Thermos. His quad bike, loaded with rolls of netting, is parked beside the fence. I am in no mood to be sociable and veer away behind a knoll towards Moel Meirch, a rough little hill where juniper, uncommon in most of Snowdonia, grows in profusion. Down below, on my right, the boggy flats at the mouth of Cwm Edno are scored by quad bike tracks, leading towards Dolwyddelan. There, too, a solitary rowan tree grows near the spot where one wild February night in 1952 a Dakota en route from London to Dublin dived nose-first into the bog with the loss of all on board. For many years the tailplane remained visible, but it has been tidied away now, and there is nothing left but a discreet plaque to indicate that this is consecrated ground.

I reach Bwlch Ehediad, an ancient pass whose boundary dykes date back to the time of Llewelyn the Great, continue into a secluded little cwm at the head of Llynnau Diwaunedd and climb steeply up on to the west ridge of Moel Siabod. A solitary walker is sitting on the closely nibbled turf eating his lunch, a reminder that I have been fasting and have had nothing to eat all day. The Pinnacle Cafe in Capel Curig becomes, all at once, a highly attractive destination and I set off on the long traverse across the lower slopes of Siabod. This is not exciting country, but it has a feel of being rarely visited, except by sheep, a place to savour the cool, clean taste of spring water and to peer behind little waterfalls and into the vivid greenness of nutrient-rich flushes for mosses and ferns.

But a walk in Snowdonia is all too often an emotional roller-coaster ride for me. The sudden aggressive roar of a low-flying jet headed for the Nant Ffrancon has scarcely died away when it is followed by the persistent drone of a helicopter flying in the opposite direction. In most parts of the world the use of aircraft for commercial or military purposes within a national park is unthinkable. Not so in Britain, where the Ministry of Defence is as impervious to criticism as any police state for all its politely worded PR. Thirty years of protest and the cession of the Cold War has led only to an increase in the number of jets screaming through the valleys. We even provide air space for pilots of other nations, forbidden to fly so low at home. As for helicopters, few can object to those of the RAF whose rescue missions have reduced the suffering of countless casualties, but the same cannot be said for the increasing numbers of civilian and army machines that pollute Snowdonia with their noise.

My mood darkens again and I descend to Capel Curig disappointed and dejected. I need food and drink, but companionship also, and reassurance that ultimately 'all shall be well'.

I suppose I am clinging to a way of thinking about wild places that is no longer tenable in the twenty-first century. Perhaps we have no choice but to abandon the notion, inherited from the Victorians, of mountains as natural cathedrals with all the spaciousness, grandeur and harmony that goes with them, and which is so hard to experience now. Instead, perhaps, we need to focus more closely, to cultivate an awareness of what our feet tread on, or our fingers grasp, to value more highly those fleeting moments of wonder, surprise or gratitude, which can spring from examining and paying attention to simple miracles like the petals of a wild flower or the iridescence on the back of a beetle.

Maybe such an approach can help us steer a middle course that is neither angry activism nor hopeless apathy, which accepts the world as it is without bitterness, yet cares enough to have some small effect on others. And can allow us still to derive pleasure and succour from going for a walk. I hope so.

On the summit of Bwlch y Groes. The Aran ridge is the skyline behind.

7

Aran End to End

On a rare fine day one October, on impulse, I drove east along the A5 to Cerrigydrudion and then headed across to Bala. Dewdrops glistened on the grass verge and the wind turbines were motionless – every one. Topping a rise, I was suddenly confronted by a sea of mist created by condensation over Llyn Tegid and, emerging from the froth like some sea monster, the dark bulk of Aran Benllyn, seen end on. Moments later I was engulfed in the fog and it was headlights on and thirty miles per hour the rest of the way through Bala and on to Llanuwchllyn.

Aran Benllyn, 884 metres, and Aran Fawddwy, 905 metres, locally referred to simply as The Aran, are the highest points of a ridge that runs twelve kilometres from Llanuwchllyn in the north to Cwm Cywarch in the south, almost eight kilometres of it over 600 metres. Although nowhere difficult or exposed, it is a long way and, with no short, simple escape routes, it would feel quite committing in a storm. In good weather, however, the views are magnificent and as a walk it is a Snowdonia classic, albeit less frequented than most.

The Snowdonia National Park is the best part of eighty kilometres from north to south and getting on for fifty east to west. Living in the Conwy valley it is easy to neglect the fine mountain country in the south and east of the Park. Recently, it had occurred to me that I had never walked the Aran ridge end to end, an omission I now hoped to rectify. Like all linear walks, transport at the end can be a problem. My solution was to leave my pushbike in the tidy little Snowdonia National Park Authority (SNPA) car park in Llanuwch-llyn and then take the long but fast and scenic route round via Brithdir to Dinas Mawddwy. From there it is but a short step to lovely Cwm Cywarch at the head of which the SNPA has created another small car park, complete with a discreet portaloo, to cater for the needs of rock climbers as well as hill-walkers. Being a Sunday, there were half a dozen cars already there, though mid-week there are often none. Two hours after leaving home I finally set off.

The path picked its way through fields of bracken beginning to rust, to follow a stream into a steep defile. Overhead wet, black crags beetled menacingly, the only sign of life a solitary raven high overhead, silhouetted against a flawless blue sky. I have fond memories of climbing here in summertime, on the firm, dry rock of long multipitch routes with cheery names like *Acheron* (one of the rivers of Hades, in Greek mythology) and *Doom*, but today they looked distinctly uninviting. When the angle finally eased the faint squelchy path divided, one branch, an old right of way continuing westwards, the other heading northeast over a boggy plateau to Aran Fawddwy. Until the Countryside Rights Of Way (CROW) Act of 2000 and the subsequent publishing of maps showing access land in 2005, this was a permissive path achieved only after long and patient negotiation by SNPA. In our national parks all land not owned by the National Trust is in private ownership and it is easy to forget that for a number of years in the eighties most of The Aran was a no-go area for hillwalkers. Enraged by gates left open, walls damaged and sheep worried by visitors' dogs, local farmers formed themselves into the Aran Society, a vigilante group who pledged to keep outsiders off the mountain. I first learned about it from a farmer who politely but firmly turned two of us away when we tried to approach the climbing crag of Gist Ddu, above Llyn Lliwbran. He had no objection himself, he said, but he would be in trouble with his neighbours if he allowed us to go on. A few years later, after the permissive path had been created, I did reach the cliff to climb a very fine route called *Aardvark*, but we had to drop in from above; there was still no access to the flanks of the mountain. Even the permissive path had limitations. We drove to Llanuwchllyn with our dog one day in the nineties only to find a large uncompromising sign saying, 'NO DOGS', on or off a lead. So it was a pleasure this time to find no aggressive signage and to know that I had a legal right, once away from the farm at the bottom, to go where I pleased.

The path followed a fence beside which someone, a National Park warden no doubt, had painstakingly placed a twin line of planks over the wet peat. These worked well, except where the planks had worked loose from the cross members beneath. When this occurred, one end of the plank smacked me on the nose while the other deposited me thigh deep in the bog. After this had happened twice and it had become clear that the path was going to follow the fence all the way to the top, I lost interest and veered away to the east. Only 300 yards away was a drier, more interesting line following the rim of the rocky headwall of Hengwm, from where the alternative path from Cywarch, which runs over the spur of Drysgol, emerged soon afterwards. The Aran is a textbook example of the effects of glaciation, the west flank being open, easy angled and poorly drained while the east, receiving more snow from prevailing westerly winds and having less sun to melt it, has been chewed into by ice, resulting in a series of small, steep-backed cwms.

A covey of grouse rose up, calling indignantly. A beautiful russet-backed kestrel arced away downwind. A steeper and rockier hillside brought me to the summit plateau and, a few hundred yards away, the trig point where several parties were picnicking. With not unlimited daylight and no lights on my bike, I pushed on picking my way carefully down a short rock step. Soon afterwards, I left the path to investigate a carefully made oval cairn which commemorates RAF pilots killed in the vicinity while training during the Second World War. The cairn is on the lip of some very steep ground from where one looks straight down on to Craiglyn Dyfi, a little lake which is the source of the river Dyfi. It is a secluded place much more often seen than actually visited. From here the river flows initially east before bending south and eventually west to enter the sea at Aberdyfi.

The rest of the ridge, it has to be said, is pleasant but unexciting, much of it once again following a fence, but this is compensated for by wide views in every direction. In front, the bright green of improved grassland with Arenig Fawr on the one hand and Llyn Tegid on the other drawing steadily closer; behind, the long dark scarp wall of Cadair Idris; to the west, isolated Rhobell Fawr, site of the volcano that kick-started the Ordovician era, and the Rhinog hills beyond; and to the east, the broad expanses of heather moorland in the Berwyn Area of Outstanding Natural Beauty (a designation much derided by Welsh politicians these days). Aran Benllyn came and went, almost unnoticed on the broad, undulating ridge and soon I was on the long gradual descent, past a lone wind turbine, to Llanuwchllyn.

Back at the bike my day was far from over. The sun was dropping but it was a still windless afternoon and, as I toiled up the long hill to the infamous Bwlch y Groes, my attention was more on the sweat pouring off my brow than on the view across Cwm Cynllwyd to the precipitous shady flank of The Aran, emerging above an intervening ridge. The other side of Bwlch y Groes is significantly steeper and, for the cyclist, definitely better taken in descent than ascent, though you would not want your brakes to fail. Although popular with visitors in the summer this road is not much used the rest of the year, except by farm vehicles, so it came as a shock, taking a sharp bend near the bottom at speed, to meet a Range Rover coming the other way. Fortunately a track on the other side of the road acted as an escape lane and all was well. As it happens, this delightful grassy track – in the autumn strewn with wax-cap fungi like red, yellow and orange buttons – leads up Llaethnant towards Craiglyn Dyfi. It can be the starting point for an alternative route up on to the Aran but, be warned, parking is very limited.

A mile further on the road was filled with milling sheep. Backlit by a westering sun, they were stopped in front of a small bridge on the far side of which three motorcyclists were waiting to go up the pass. Blithely unaware of either them or me, an elderly farmer sat astride his quad bike lighting his pipe. It did not seem the time or the place to be in a hurry and I enjoyed simply watching the scene. Eventually, the pipe was lit, a Border collie moved the sheep on and three middle-aged bank managers in leathers came past looking sternly ahead. Taking to the verge I managed to squeeze past the sheep, but had to stop a few hundred yards later to clear bracken and nettles from my chain-wheel. Feeling distinctly well exercised now, I pedalled on down the valley to where the Cywarch stream joins the Dyfi for the final four-kilometre pull up to the car. I had closed the circle around the Aran on wheels as well as traversing it end to end on foot. An ambition achieved, it had been a deeply satisfying mountain day, one to savour and relive on the journey home.

Paved trackway at Pont Scethin in the heart of Ardudwy.

8

Awheel in Ardudwy

Lying west of the Rhinogydd Mountains, between Harlech and Barmouth, the region of Ardudwy has always been a favourite stamping ground of mine. The strip of land between the main road and the sea was sacrificed years ago to the caravans and campsites of the holiday industry, but the rough pasture inland running up to the even rougher Rhinog mountains remains surprisingly empty, even in the holiday season. It is also, in the words of archaeologist Peter Crew, 'one of the richest ancient landscapes in Britain', redolent of human activity stretching back thousands of years. Thanks to a network of roads and tracks, many of the latter dating back to prehistoric times, it lends itself to exploration on a bike.

One day at the end of May, when the land was finally warming up after a long cold winter, I left the car in Tal y Bont and set off uphill. Tracks and bridleways led through dappled woodland of oak and beech, their leaves a kaleidoscope of soft, fresh green; bluebells beneath positively throbbed with colour and little streams flashed in the sunlight. The air was loud with the song of blackbird, thrush and chaffinch. A flick of red tail feathers betrayed a redstart. After weeks of poor weather, it all felt quite idyllic. The bridleway joined a narrow tarmac road, emerging from the trees near Cors Gedol Hall, an Elizabethan manor house now a hotel specialising in wedding receptions. Passing through a gate, I came to the remains of a cromlech, inconspicuous beneath a pair of hawthorn trees and backed by colourful flowering gorse. It is a delightful spot. A huge capstone, some three metres by two rests on two stumpy uprights and is surrounded by stone from the cairn that must have completely covered it five thousand years ago or more. Traces of the fields and huts of the Neolithic community that built it can still be found on the other side of the road, among more recent settlements of post-Roman and medieval epochs.

Back-tracking as far as the gate, I continued uphill on a stony track, in low gear, wheatears flitting everywhere along ubiquitous dry stone walls. At a junction of trackways a new-looking signpost informed me that I was on the Ardudwy Way, a walking route from Barmouth to Harlech. Crossing a broad ridge the modern water-board track continues northwards to Llyn Bodlyn. I took the line of a much older route, heading down a boggy hillside scarred by deep vehicle ruts filled with water, the first discordant note of the day. Ahead lay a small, hump-backed bridge over the stream which flows out of Bodlyn, Pont Scethin, the heart of what Jim Perrin once described as, 'one of the most fragile and exquisite landscapes of a country of exquisite and fragile natural beauty'. Although only a few kilometres from the busy coast road, it felt very quiet and remote. Where better to pause for a picnic, sheltered by the parapet from a strong east wind? The stonework of the bridge was brightened by yellow hawkweed and, as I stooped to drink from the stream, weed glimmered green-gold through the water. The dipper I had expected to find was nowhere to be seen but a pair of agitated wagtails made it clear that I was an unwelcome intruder.

Received wisdom has it that this bridge was once on a coach road from Harlech to Dolgellau but I find this hard to believe. At its apex the arched bridge is barely two-metres wide and the section of road through boggy ground just beyond it is paved with stone slabs barely a metre wide, reminiscent of the so called Roman steps in Cwm Bychan. It seems much more likely that bridge and paving, like the Roman steps, were part of a medieval packhorse trail and that stagecoach passengers would have been obliged to walk or ride on horseback for this section of their journey.

Beyond the slabs the track starts to climb and for 200 metres it is a washed out jumble of eroded stone. Things improve at a hairpin bend to the right and soon after one passes a now barely legible memorial to Janet Haigh, 'who even as late as her eighty-forth year, despite dim sight and stiffened joints still loved to walk this way from Tal y Bont to Penmaenpool'. She must have been a redoubtable lady but on reaching the crest of the ridge, well over 500 metres above sea level, it is easy to see why she loved it so. To the north, one looks back across Ardudwy and the Moelwynion to the Snowdon massif; to the west lie the waters of Cardigan Bay bounded by the long, lumpy profile of the Llyn Peninsula. Ahead, over the Mawddach estuary, is the undulating northern escarpment of Cadair Idris, crying out to be walked in its entirety from Cross Foxes to Llanfihangel y Pennant. There can be few finer viewpoints in the whole of Wales.

Here the trail skirts the head of a small cwm before descending the long armlike ridge of Braich. Twenty years ago this was an almost unmarked green road that gave an exhilarating, swooping, carefree descent. Today, notices indicate that motorbikes are forbidden but the track for long distances on both sides of the pass has been gouged into tram rails several inches deep and the width of a trials-bike tyre, potentially lethal on a pushbike. While mountain bikes cannot be entirely blameless, all the evidence points to the damage being done by motorised bikes.

Nearly 300 metres lower I reached a meeting of ways where a small tarmac road descends to Bont Ddu on the Mawddach and paths and tracks lead east into Cwm Mynach. Instead, I took a sunken rocky trail leading west to Bwlch y Rhiwgr, which translates as Pass of the Drovers. Herds of cattle, driven for hundreds of years from Ardudwy to Dolgellau at the start of the long journey to Smithfield market, took not the well-graded track that I toiled up on my bike but a twisting grassy furrow that plunges straight down the hill from the pass. Unruly cattle are no respecters of zigzags. By the same token, they would not have been welcome in villages, which is why drovers from Llanbedr or Harlech usually took the high-level inland route, followed now by the Ardudwy Way. Be that as it may, Bwlch y Rhiwgyr is not an enjoyable ride on a bike, too steep and eroded on both sides for me. However, once the angle eases, back in Ardudwy, the old drove road becomes muddy but rideable following a nineteenth century enclosure wall across the hillside. Only a few hundred metres away is the National Trust's historically fascinating circular walk from Egryn Abbey which takes in the Iron Age hill fort of Pen y Dinas, passes close to the Neolithic burial chambers of Carneddau Hengwm, visits a Bronze Age cairn circle and descends back towards the coast by way of an extensive medieval settlement.

A prominent clump of Scots pine marks an abrupt change in the character of the landscape, from bare open sheepwalk to mixed woodland filling the valley of the Afon Ysgethin. The river is crossed by way of Pontfadog, a traditional stone bridge bearing the date 1762 which, unlike Pont Scethin, could easily have been crossed by a stagecoach. A few metres further on is the cottage of Llety Logr, known to have been an overnight stopping place for drovers and their animals. Here I left the road to follow a bridleway down through the woods close to the rushing, tumbling, white-water river, back to Tal y Bont and the twenty-first century.

Looking across the empty expanse of Waun y Griafolen, the source of the Mawddach.

9

Mawddach Source to Sea

On the map, the source of the Afon Mawddach seems an unremarkable place. Four hundred metres above sea level, Waun y Griafolen, Moor of the Rowan Tree, is a shallow basin roughly two kilometres square. Widely spaced contours seamed by sinuous blue threads imply terrain moist underfoot where peat has had ample opportunity to accumulate. The name is something of a mystery, not because today there is not a tree to be seen, unless one counts the topmost branches of some distant Sitka spruce, but because for the last three thousand years this is a place where, without sheep, willow and alder would have thrived rather than rowan. Who knows, perhaps the name derived from the drier ground of Cefn y Griafolen, a ridge of higher land to the west. On the flanks of this ridge, overlooking the moor, are traces of huts and fields which must surely date back to the warmer, drier days of the Bronze Age. It seems quite possible that the ridge, or even the settlement, could have given its name to the moor, rather than the other way round.

On the ground, Waun y Griafolen is characterised chiefly by meadow pipits and the white flower heads of cotton grass. To the south, the view is dominated by the rocks of that rough little hill Dduallt; in the south-east the long undulating ridge of Aran Benllyn peers over the skyline. Otherwise, there is not much to see, at first glance anyway, beyond tussocky grass and some eroding peat hags. It is unspectacular country and certainly not easy walking. Its charm lies in quietness and emptiness, rare commodities in the twenty-first century. Although not all that far from tarmac either to east or west, it feels remote and little visited with none of the redundant fencing and deeply gouged quad-bike tracks that disfigure so much of upland Wales. It has that quality of 'left-aloneness' that Clyde Holmes sought to capture in his paintings and poems of Cwm Hesgin, not a million miles away near Bala.

Near the twin pools that the map calls Llyn Grych-y-Waun, a multitude of streamlets coalesce to become the Mawddach, which promptly drops through a steep gorge into Cwm yr Allt Lwyd. This is a rather forlorn little valley where no one now lives even though there are some substantial farmsteads not yet beyond repair. At this point, for the traveller bent on reaching the sea at Barmouth in a day, a bike becomes an attractive option making short work of the four kilometres to Abergeirw.

Despite featuring on signposts all the way from Dolgellau in the south and from Bronaber in the northwest, there is nothing at Abergeirw but a couple of houses, a tiny chapel and a postbox. A weary traveller in need of sustenance would be sorely disappointed. It is, however, the gateway to the sixteen-thousand acres of land dedicated to the growing of trees, mostly coniferous, which was given the name Coed y Brenin, or King's Wood, in 1935, the silver jubilee of King George V. Nowadays, it is known as Coed y Brenin Forest Park acknowledging its statutory role in providing for recreation and amenity as well as the growing of timber. In places, especially lower down near Ganllwyd, where stands of Douglas fir have been given space and are being allowed to tower upwards, it is at last beginning to resemble a forest rather than a plantation.

At this point the cyclist is obliged to leave the river for a while and a certain pioneering spirit is required to find and negotiate bridleways that are boldly marked on the map but less obvious on the ground, through trees and over fields, past the recently abandoned smallholding of Tyddyn Mawr, back to the rushing waters of the Mawddach.

Progress becomes more rapid on good forest tracks and in no time the surviving sheds of Gwynfynydd Gold Mine heave into view on the other side of the river. This was controversially reopened in the early nineties and when – to no one's surprise – gold proved elusive, it was run for a time as a tourist attraction before closing again in 1999. Undoubtedly, 'there's gold in them thar hills', and to this day the occasional enthusiast can be found panning by the side of the river. But once the initial feverish excitement of the great gold rush of 1860 had subsided, gold mining has never proved commercially viable for any length of time. Let's hope it stays that way.

Tourism, on the other hand, has been a source of jobs and income since the eighteenth century when a taste for the picturesque and the sublime in landscape became fashionable. The wars of the French Revolution and the Napoleonic era, which put Europe off limits for nearly thirty years, encouraged even more visitors to come to gaze in rapture at the spray-filled gorges and tumbling white water of the Mawddach Falls and the nearby Pistyll Cain. For most of the nineteenth and twentieth centuries these waterfalls were among the premier tourist destinations of Wales. Today, however, the centre of attention has shifted to the visitor centre on the river Eden, just off the A470, Wales' north-south trunk road. With riverside walks, a children's playground and a coffee shop as well as running trails and mountain-bike routes of all levels of difficulty, it has become hugely popular and a major money-spinner for what was the Forestry Commission (now part of Natural Resources Wales).

Below Ganllwyd the road becomes tarmac and the cyclist bowls along faster than ever until unexpectedly forced to change down a few gears where the road climbs above the ruins of Cymer Abbey. The abbey was built in 1198 by Cistercian monks and ten years later it was granted a charter by Llywelyn the Great giving it the right to graze animals, take fish from the river and extract minerals and timber from the hills all the way from Barmouth to above Dolgellau. Nowadays the site is managed by CADW (the quango responsible for cultural heritage in Wales), though so smothered by tents and caravans in summer that it is hard to gain any sense of what life must have been like there.

A little further downstream the Mawddach, which has already been swelled by the Cain and the Eden, sizeable rivers in their own right, is joined by the Wnion coming in from Dolgellau. Here it becomes tidal and salty and meanders through reed beds to Penmaenpool, the name immortalised by Gerard Manley Hopkins who wrote a charming poem for the visitors' book in the inn. The cyclist must negotiate the main road to pick up the old railway line which is now a multi-use trail very popular with dog walkers and pram pushers as well as cyclists at all time of year.

At Penmaenpool is the George III pub, a welcome source of refreshment, and an interesting SNPA information centre in the old signal box, sadly open only in the summer. It is hard to imagine now, but sea-going ships were being built here from local timber during the first half of the nineteenth century to transport roofing slates over to Ireland and up the coast to Liverpool for export. On the other side of the river lies Cwm Mynach, or Monk's Valley, much of it now owned by the Woodland Trust and the site of a long-term project to replace Sitka spruce with native hardwoods. The name is a reminder that until the Reformation in the sixteenth century all this land was managed by and for the monks of Cymer Abbey. The valley can be reached in a car by paying to cross the toll bridge or by driving round six kilometres on the main road.

On a bike, the final few kilometres to the sea are a delight. Even at speed one can hear the chatter of sedge warblers in the reeds and spot the black heads of reed buntings. Out on the mud flats, herons stand sentinel every few yards it seems, and curlew stalk about probing the mud with their long curved bills. On the water, shelduck are easily distinguished by their size and black and white appearance from afar. At Morfa Mawddach station one is on the Cambrian railway line and can catch a train coming from Pwllheli to Machynlleth and thence to Aberystwyth or the other way to Shrewsbury and on to Birmingham. A more satisfying conclusion to the journey, however, is to pedal over the wooden boards of the walkway on the railway bridge to the tea shops of Barmouth, pausing on the way to look over the sand bars and wooded flanks of the estuary to the dark north face of Cadair Idris.

Nick Dixon on *Cascade*, Craig y Rhaeadr, in the Llanberis Pass.

10

Snowdon in Winter

With ice-honed arêtes radiating in all directions, embracing high-backed cwms and dark, glacial lakes, Snowdon is easily the finest mountain in Wales, and superior to those in England, come to that. More's the pity then that, in summer, its summit is thronged by the one-hundred-and-fifty people who arrive every hour by train and the almost equal number who arrive in the same space of time on foot, while the air is fouled by a cocktail of coal and diesel.

In winter, however, a metamorphosis occurs. Close the cafe, smother the landscape in snow, and Snowdon becomes again a magnificent mountain. Like the onset of night, the quiet, persistent falling of snow quickly transforms the most familiar scene into a place that is strange, mysterious, and sometimes dangerous. Railway line, paths, boulder fields, streams and ponds all disappear under a white blanket, a blanket that, far from being smooth and uniform, startles in the infinite range of delicate forms and textures created by the play of wind or sun on its surface.

For the mountaineer, the arrival of winter means the dusting down of a whole new set of equipment, techniques and attitudes. For while snow is more accommodating than rock when it comes to fashioning a comfortable stance on which to stand, or even a handhold to pull on if the snow is too soft for a pick, it is also less strong and more liable to give way unexpectedly. Hard snow, without crampons or an ice axe, and the ability to use them, is a very smooth, unforgiving surface on which to slip, and breaking trail in deep soft snow to somewhere like the Trinity Face of Clogwyn y Garnedd, beneath the summit of Yr Wyddfa, can be an exhausting labour quite different to summer walking.

The Trinity Face normally appeals more to the botanist than to the climber but like other damp, vegetated crags such as Ysgolion Duon and Twll Du, it provides excellent winter climbing. Facing north at 1,000 metres above sea level, snow lingers here even when it has long vanished from the nether regions. Here, countless climbers have been introduced to the arts of step-kicking and step-cutting, cramponing and ice axe braking. Difficulty varies wildly according to conditions. With a good build-up of snow, Central Trinity gully must be skiable. Yet one spring day, when there was barely a snow patch to be seen from the road, it gave 200 metres of perfect cramponing, including thirty metres of technical climbing up a ribbon of water ice. On another occasion, with much more snow but poor visibility, having climbed the right-hand gully, Jeremy Light and I chose to descend Central Trinity. Halfway down, at the Narrows, we met a large party on their way up. A closer look revealed a group of five, all in city shoes or trainers, with not an axe between them. In the mist, they had followed the wrong set of footprints (probably ours) and lost the Miners' Track. After teetering up a hundred metres of steepening snow, the leader had encountered hard ice and was pawing at it ineffectually with his smooth-soled shoes. His friends were lined up below, one behind the other, like dominoes. We arrived with a rope just in time.

However, my first acquaintance with Clogwyn y Garnedd was on a day when we saw not a soul. It was midweek, one November. There was plenty of snow about but it was drizzling at Pen y Pass and cloud had settled on Glaslyn. Wind was rushing about noisily among the crags. It was only some curious perversity that impelled us onward as we stomped up a slushy

Miners' Track into the mist. More by luck than judgement, we groped our way through the mines to the big snow slope of the Trinities, located a shelf slanting leftwards and found ourselves at the foot of a corner with a slabby right wall blotched with snow. This was Snowdrop, described by the guide as containing, 'one of the finest steep snow pitches in Wales'. The slab demanded delicate cramponing, axe and feet carefully placed where the ice was thickest, until fifty feet up the corner was capped by a small roof. A lot of digging unearthed a chockstone runner from which to bridge up with confidence beneath the overhang. Reaching tentatively over the top, picks bit deeply into firm snow, all things became possible and, with a heave, the crux was behind. Ian led through up a shallow gully, which weaved its way through easier, hoar-encrusted rocks to open snow slopes and an angry wind, which sought to hurl us back down the way we had come. A few metres further and, huge and unexpected through the mist, the deserted cairn was before us.

If the Trinity Face of Yr Wyddfa has always been a popular venue for the initiation of winter climbers, the cliffs of Y Lliwedd, only a few-hundred metres away, are definitely no place for the tyro. Nearly 300 metres high, with little drainage on which ice can form, they are more of a rock-climber's playground; though even in summer, the holds slope awkwardly, the largest of blocks can be loose, and belays and protection are not easy to find. In winter, the three prominent gullies are the main attractions and all three, even with modern equipment, are serious climbs. Ice screws are of no use here. Balance and finesse are more important than the biceps and calf muscles needed for columns of pure ice, pushing rather than pulling the technique most needed. Slanting Gully has the distinction of a cave halfway up where King Arthur's knights lie fast asleep awaiting a summons in the hour of Britain's greatest need. The cave is little more than a shallow scoop, but ice usually forms only on its outer rim and thinly at that, so the climber has no choice but to sidle past awkwardly without disturbing anyone.

By contrast, on the other side of Crib y Ddysgl, down in the Llanberis Pass, are climbs in the modern idiom. On the wet rocks of Craig y Rhaeadr, cliff of the waterfall, vertical pillars of blue ice form readily. Even now, in the days of climate change, these icefalls usually form once or twice a winter, if briefly, and then queues of frustrated ice climbers quickly appear at the bottom. These climbs require strength, skill and experience to lead safely, but complete beginners can, and do, bludgeon their way up on the end of a tight rope.

But perhaps the most inspiring way to experience Snowdon in winter is to walk the justly famous Horseshoe. The traverse of Crib Goch and Crib y Ddysgl needs only a fall of snow to seem like an alpine expedition. The story is often told of the Swiss guide Melchior Anderegg, invited to stay at Pen y Pass one winter before the First World War, and who was totally deceived by the scale. Arriving on the first summit of Crib Goch, he counselled immediate retreat if the party was to avoid benightment. His client assured him it would take no more than an hour and a half to reach Yr Wyddfa, and he was correct almost to the minute. But, if the scale is not alpine, a lapse of concentration can still be fatal. It is all too easy to trip or catch a crampon point in a trouser leg or, without crampons, simply to slip and be unable to stop. The Llanberis rescue team is invariably busy on fine weekends in wintertime.

However, 'look well to each step', as Whymper cautioned all those years ago, and there can be few more exhilarating places than the summit ridge of Crib Goch in winter. The sudden exposure of the notorious knife-edge can be startling even for the experienced; the black, iceberg-studded waters of Llydaw beckoning far below. The whole of Snowdonia lies revealed, from Glyderau and Carneddau in the north, to twin-headed Arenig Fawr and the Arans in the east, to the long undulating ridge of Cadair Idris in the south. Sometimes, in cold, clear conditions, the white hills of Wicklow can dance like a mirage on the horizon, far away in the west. On occasion, the shouts of climbers on Lliwedd can carry clearly in the frozen air right across Cwm Dyli. But start at first light, which in winter is not so very early, and the chances are the mountain will be deserted, the only sound the scrunch of frozen snow underfoot. The summit will be still and silent, a place for reflection, a time to be grateful. Mountain moments do not come any better.

Jim Buckley running up Y Garn with Llyn y Cwn and Glyder Fawr in the background.

11

Mountain Running

I have been running over the hills all my life; well the last forty years, anyway. I count myself exceedingly fortunate to be still doing so, albeit at a more modest pace than yesteryear. 'Of course, you're not a real fell runner', a friend once told me, because I did not compete every weekend in organised events. Once or twice a year and the occasional mountain marathon, until they became too big, was quite enough for me. But for over ten years, running was actually a form of transport. In the days when we could not afford two cars, it was frequently useful if I ran to or from work, from Glasgwm near Penmachno to Capel Curig over two interven-ing ridges, or ran one way and biked the other. For a family man running was also a way of both taking some exercise and garnering the inspiration of high places in a short time frame. In two or three hours the fell runner can cover ground which would normally be a day's walk. Above all, running was and is, for me, a form of mountaineering and as such not without risk. Over the years I have had a few close calls involving hypothermia, low blood sugar and benightment, which have been salutary reminders that even Welsh hills can bite, but also that this is adventure, not athletics.

Nowadays I am content mostly to run around, or over, Tal y Fan, our local hill, but in days gone by I used to combine running with climbing, carrying a pair of rock shoes in a bum bag. The possibilities are endless for what the French call *enchaînements*, though preferably without the helicopters. I had a fine day's exploration once, visiting two crags new to me on a mountain I did not often visit. Leaving the car near Betws Garmon, I was able to link *Adam Rib*, an exposed and exciting Severe in quiet Cwm Du on one side of Mynydd Mawr, with *Angel Pavement*, a classic V. Diff, nowadays elevated to Hard Severe, up Craig y Bera on the other. As access to *Angel Pavement* was made problematic by a belligerent farmer, approaching from above was convenient. The highlight was pulling over a short, steep wall to find myself eyeballing a startled peregrine, a mere three metres away. The summit was a springy sward of bilberry, crowberry and cowberry, flecked white with the perversely named reindeer-moss lichen. It had been dried and warmed by the sun all day and cried out to be lain upon, full length, for a few blissful minutes of quiet. I was almost asleep when a large party of ramblers arrived and I had to stir myself. Then I freewheeled gladly round in a horseshoe down to Llyn Cwellyn, at the bottom passing beneath the bristling overhangs of the wolf's lair, Castell Cidwm. There was no bridge at the outflow so the river had to be waded. On the far side was a large sign facing the other way. I knew what it would say, so I didn't bother looking.

Another time, one of those crisp, early summer mornings when the blue of the lakes and the green of the low-lying fields were almost unbelievable, as if digitally enhanced, I ran up the Pony Track on Cadair Idris and along the faint traverse path to Llyn y Gadair. A few unexpectedly steep moves above *The Table* and some spectacular positions at the top, saw me up *Cyfrwy Arête* where Sir Arnold Lunn came to grief all those years ago. Continuing over the jumbled rocks of Pen y Gadair and past the summit shelter, a carefree grassy ridge led to Mynydd Moel, then cautious running through steep bluffs, down to the dark waters of Llyn Cau. The way home was up *Pencoed Pillar*, given three-star status in the guidebook, but really an exercise in scaling vertical heather and steep wet rushes, if the truth be known – but fun, nonetheless. As I came bounding back down the path to the car park, dressed only in a pair of shorts, sweat streaming off me; I met an elderly couple with a spaniel toiling upwards. 'Doing a spot of fell-running, then?' the man asked cheerfully. I could only laugh with delight and hurtle on my way. I was back home for lunch.

One of the most memorable days I ever had in Wales was in a grey cold spell one October, perfect for running but cold on the fingers for climbing. Starting later than intended, I walked up to the bwlch above Ffynnon Llugwy with Netti and a friend, dropped down to the start of *Amphitheatre Buttress* and rejoined them for a quick coffee on the summit of Carnedd Llewelyn. Running on towards Dafydd and down to Ffynnon Lloer and the A5, I found *Grooved Arête* on Tryfan for once deserted. *Tennis Shoe* on the Idwal Slabs was followed by *Lazarus* and that nasty little *Groove Above*, reaching the top of the Glyders by way of the almost alpine *Central Arête*. The plan had been to finish on Lliwedd but now I realised there was only time to visit Cyrn Las. It had been an enjoyable but uneventful day, until that point on Main Wall where you move left round an arête on to a steep wall, overhanging a deep, dark gully, a lot of space beneath your feet. It must be one of the most exposed pitches in Wales. As I stepped round, my fingers reached that degree of cold where it is hard to tell whether you really have a firm grip or not, when even large holds don't feel quite large or in-cut enough.

I made the moves in the end; but there were a few moments in which I was uncomfortably aware that there was not another soul in Cwm Glas, that there was not long till dark, that there were many metres of air beneath me, and that I didn't much fancy down-climbing what I had come up. Adrenaline took me most of the way up on to Crib y Ddysgl, then gravity took over and I jogged easily down the zigzags to Glaslyn, Snowdon hulking hugely overhead. A big, yellow moon, rising in the east, helpfully lit the way back to Pen y Pass.

The Pen y Gwryd Hotel.

12

Pen y Gwryd Memories

My earliest recollection of the Pen y Gwryd hotel dates from the mid-sixties when I was a teenager. My brother and I had hitchhiked up to north Wales and were camped at 'Willie's farm', Gwern Gof Uchaf, in the Ogwen valley. We had climbed one day on the Milestone Buttress and on another battled our way up one of the long routes on the east face of Tryfan. On the day in question, we set out for the cliffs of Glyder Fach. The cloud was right down and visibility so limited that we might never have found the crag, let alone climbed anything. As it was, we had reached Llyn Bochlwyd and had struck out away from the path that leads to Bwlch Tryfan, when we heard a whistle blowing somewhere high above. We recognised it as a call for help and, forgetting about our compass bearing, if we had one, we headed upwards. The terrain became steeper and steeper, the visibility worse and worse until we could scarcely see each other, and the insistent whistling never seemed to get any closer. We continued onwards and upwards interminably, conscious that we had absolutely no idea where we were, until eventually the angle began to ease and we guessed that we were approaching the plateau of Glyder Fach. Only now did the whistle sound fairly close and then, quite suddenly, a few yards ahead, we found a little cluster of people. Their faces lit up at the sight of us but when they realised we were not the rescue team their expressions crumpled with disappointment. It was a school party, one of whose members had collapsed with hypothermia, in those days known as 'exposure', brought on by cold wet conditions. It was the sort of incident that was becoming all too common and led a few years later to the establishment of the Mountain Leader training scheme. Fortunately for the boys and their teacher – and for Kiff and me as well, come to that – the real rescue team arrived from the opposite direction moments later. Its members were all large men exuding confidence and competence and in no time the casualty had been manoeuvered into a sleeping bag and lashed on to a stretcher. Kiff and I were handed a carrying strap each and shown how to pass it over one shoulder to take the weight and off we went. We very soon discovered that carrying a stretcher down a rocky, wet hillside, even with plenty of carriers, is an exhausting business. It felt as though we had been slipping and sliding downhill for hours when, abruptly, we dropped out of the cloud to see a road and a cluster of buildings not far below. It was Pen y Gwryd.

The casualty was loaded into an ambulance, the school group had already been escorted off the hill and we, as members of the rescue team, were ushered into the bar and found ourselves clutching pints of bitter, on the house. I do not remember any faces specifically but I suspect that it was the first and only time that I met Chris Briggs, mine host of the Pen y Gwryd Hotel and mountain rescue supremo of North Wales at the time. At that age beer was not much to our taste and when a friendly policeman offered to drive us the twelve kilometres back round to Ogwen, we put down our glasses without regret and headed for the squad car. Fifty years on, I find myself a trainee member of the Ogwen Valley Mountain Rescue team, struggling sometimes with the sheer technicality of modern rescue.

Not long after that, I met Esme Kirby for the first time. Esme lived in Dyffryn Mymbyr farm midway between Plas y Brenin and Pen y Gwryd and was a close friend of the Briggs family. I was coming down off the

Glyders one day and found myself confronted by a stone wall barring access to the main road. I had just climbed over it when an elderly Morris 1000 pulled up alongside. A diminutive figure emerged, bristling with indignation. 'Young man, have you any idea how much I have to spend repairing my walls every year?', she demanded. 'One hundred and fifty pounds' (at least £2,000 today), she continued, before I could open my mouth, and proceeded to berate me for several minutes before driving off, leaving me thoroughly chastened. Not only had she made it clear that she was extremely angry but, more to the point, she made me understand why. There was no room for excuses but she never became abusive either. I could only apologise humbly and promise to be much more careful in the future about where and how I crossed walls. I have never forgotten the effectiveness of that reprimand and I have kept my promise.

It was only a matter of time before I read *I Bought a Mountain* by Thomas Firbank and realised that I had fallen foul of its heroine but our paths did not cross again until the seventies. By then I was married, with three small children, and living in North Wales. By chance, I picked up a flyer about the Snowdonia National Park Society, which Esme had founded in 1967, and felt that I should support its work. I was never a very active member but Esme used to ring up from time to time enquiring about National Park issues in the Penmachno area and up on the Migneint, or to ask me to write a letter of objection regarding some undesirable development. On a couple of occasions I was invited round to Society HQ in her kitchen at Dyffryn, a low-ceilinged room with tiny windows set in thick stone walls which made it seem dark whatever the time of day. Every conceivable work surface was piled high with books, reports and papers. Cooking was clearly a low priority.

In 1989, the Snowdonia Society (as it became, to avoid confusion with the National Park Authority) bought Ty Hyll, the Ugly House, where the A5 crosses the river Llugwy mid-way between Betws y Coed and Capel Curig, and converted it into an office. Sadly, this was the start of an increasingly acrimonious conflict with Esme, who could not bear to relinquish the reins of the society she had founded, and a committee who found her style too confrontational and wanted the society to be run by a paid director. Four directors came and went in quick succession, quite unable to work with Esme, until finally a bad-tempered extraordinary general meeting in 1992 saw her replaced by David Firth as Chairman.

Many of Esme's friends, including Jo Briggs and her daughter Jane Pullee, immediately resigned from the Society and the well-meaning David Firth was *persona non grata* at the Pen y Gwryd hotel for years afterwards.

For myself, I still liked and admired Esme on a personal level but I could see that if the Snowdonia Society was to be an effective pressure group on behalf of the national park, a willingness to negotiate and sometimes compromise was essential. Today the society's office is at the Caban in Bryn Refail from where it continues to monitor inappropriate planning applications, respond to government policy documents and organise a range of conservation work within the park with a team of hardy volunteers. Ty Hyll is still owned by the society and is open to the public as a tearoom and honeybee interpretation centre, along with its delightful wildlife garden and surrounding woodland.

You cannot live in North Wales for any length of time without some contact with Pen y Gwryd. Usually for me, it was calling in for a drink after a day's climbing in the pass but more than once I found myself giving a lift to pretty Danish chambermaids hitching to or from the metropolis of Betws y Coed on their afternoon off. Once, Netti and I stayed the night after a party and marvelled at the antique shared bathroom and accommodation little changed since the days of the Everesters. Another time, during the making of a Channel 4 production, we came down from a wet, murky Crib Goch to be filmed reviewing the day in the cosy little snug behind the bar.

Another link was Chris Brasher whom I knew initially through running mountain marathons and later as a trustee of the John Muir Trust. Chris was always keen for the trust to buy a property in Wales (an ambition that has still not been achieved despite several attempts) and I remember a convivial dinner which he hosted at Pen y Gwryd for trustees to meet friends like John Disley, John Jackson and Peter Kirby. Chris was well known as an athlete, journalist and entrepreneur and was something of an *habitué* at the Pen y Gwryd as he owned a holiday cottage in Nant Gwynant for many years. He was also a good friend of Esme Kirby and it was he who stumped up the cash to buy and then demolish the derelict filling station at Pen y Gwryd, an eyesore that had been the *bête noir* of both Esme and the Briggs family for years.

Chris had always been an advocate of the Shipton/Tilman lightweight approach to mountaineering; in particular he was fond of Tilman's famous dictum that any expedition worth going on could be 'organised on the back of an envelope'. From this grew the OBOE club, a disparate but sociable group of Chris's friends who would gather from time to time for a weekend's walking in the hills. I enjoyed a number of these events but could not help wondering, sometimes, if Tilman would have approved the amount of telephoning required to organise them. On one occasion Chris employed me professionally to guide the party through the underground caverns of Wrysgan Mine above Tanygrisiau and then across the Moelwyns to Nant Gwynant. All went well until, just as the rain set in, Chris chose to lead us on a fearsome bush-bash through a rhododendron thicket in search of his old house. At some point he must have communicated with Pen y Gwryd, unbeknownst to me. (It was very early days for mobile phones but I knew Chris owned one, literally the size of a house-brick, because the previous winter he had insisted on stopping in the middle of a ski tour in the French Alps to check on how his racehorse was doing at Newmarket). Just as we were resigning ourselves to a weary trudge up the valley, Brian and Jane Pullee appeared in their big white Mercedes and another car. Their arrival, like fairy godparents, was as welcome as it was unexpected. Uncomplaining, they conveyed us, dripping and muddy, to the warmth and hospitality of their remarkable hotel.

Llangelynin Old Church in the hills behind Conwy.

13

Coming Home

Recently, I came home after some weeks' ski touring among the peaks and glaciers of the Swiss Alps. One day I was breakfasting in a cloud-wrapped hut at 3,200 metres, the next I was eating bread and cheese for lunch on the terrace outside our house in the lower Conwy valley. My nearest and dearest were out so I wandered a few metres up the lane and took the sunken track that slants steeply up the hillside.

It was May, the loveliest of months in North Wales. The big ash trees were still bare skeletons outlined against a blue sky, but every other tree and plant was vibrant with life and colour. Sunlight filtered through fresh young oak leaves so varied in hue that the word green became laughable, dappling the earthy track beneath. Primroses glimmered from the shady bank. In the wood below were celandine and stitchwort, glowing drifts of bluebells and, along the banks of the little stream, sprawling masses of golden saxifrage. The thick scent of wild garlic lay heavy in the air.

The mosaic of tiny fields above the track are less open land than clearings in a wood. I picked my way up them, conscious of the sounds of spring everywhere – the urgent bleating of lambs for their mothers, the mewing of a pair of buzzards circling slowly overhead, the bright treble of a robin advertising its territory, the mellow contralto of a blackbird, the unvarying two-tone call of a chiffchaff, and, further away, the long trills of a wood warbler. For years I have recognised that song without ever actually seeing the bird, or not clearly enough to be sure, just the occasional tantalising glimpse of a brown shape flitting from bush to bush.

I sat down to enjoy the view over the Conwy estuary and across to the distant turrets of the castle. Lying back in the grass, I shut my eyes and savoured the gentle warmth of the sun, so friendly after the bright, reflected light and burning glare of high altitudes. There is nowhere in the world I would rather be in spring than this miniature, antique land of Wales; and there is no surer way to heighten that appreciation and quicken the senses than a sojourn in the dramatic, beautiful but essentially sterile world of the High Alps.

The life of a mountain guide can seem an endless cycle of leave-takings and homecomings – an incomprehensible lifestyle to others. Yet the rewards are many, not least the opportunity presented by coming home. Over the years the farewells have become, perhaps, slightly easier, but coming home never fails to stir feelings of anticipation, gratitude, and a sense of renewal in relationship to places as well as to loved ones. Never was an aphorism truer than absence makes the heart grow fonder. Yet often it goes beyond that. Coming home can be like waking up. Familiar faces and familiar scenes have an immediacy and vividness usually absent. So much of the time perceptions are dulled by preoccupation and everyday cares so that people and places and things are seen only, as 'through a glass darkly'. For me, at any rate, moments of real clarity are rare and valuable.

The Hollandia hut, perched on a wind-blasted col high in the Bernese Oberland, had felt like a microcosm of the European Community. I was guiding a group of Dutch skiers. Steve Jones was there with two Danish clients. There was a Swiss guide with some Americans. There were parties of Swiss and French and some cheery Spaniards. Unexpectedly, a foot of snow had fallen overnight and at dawn there was still nothing to be seen from the windows but the occasional snowflake. Breakfast of stale bread and instant coffee was a livelier affair than usual as options were discussed and plans revised. We waited awhile hoping for a clearance but when we finally left it was in thick cloud that would have been true whiteout but for the tracks left by Steve's party, skiing roped, an hour earlier. Halfway down the glacier, however, we dropped out of it and could enjoy untracked powder briefly before the snow became wet, heavy and difficult with decreasing altitude. As we descended the narrow, steep-sided Lötschental, we came across more and more evidence of catastrophic avalanche activity earlier in the year; forested hillsides where every tree had been snapped at half height by wind blast, tree trunks and the smashed wreckage of buildings poking out of mountains of debris, twisted pieces of metal from guard rails and bridges. The road, normally clear at this time of year, was nowhere to be seen.

It was a reminder, if a reminder was needed, that big mountains, like bulls, are unpredictable, always potentially hostile. I can never feel totally at home in glaciated country. As a guide, I have learned that you cannot afford to drop your guard at any time in the Alps. We are allowed to be there temporarily, on sufferance, permitted glimpses of the unnerving power and dangerous beauty that make mountains sacred in so many cultures, but comfortable and at ease we can never be, unless we are asking for trouble. By contrast, the hills of Snowdonia, from which the ice disappeared ten thousand years ago and where life flourishes even on the summits if you look for it – these are hills where I do feel at home.

I opened my eyes and looked around. The wood warbler was closer now, insistent, but elusive as ever. A grey squirrel, a few yards away at the foot of an oak, was watching intently, stock-still except for a tail that rotated madly. I moved ever so slightly and it shot up the tree, only to creep down the far side and peer cautiously round the trunk. Suddenly, out of the corner of my eye, I caught a flicker of movement. Slowly, carefully, I raised the binoculars and there, on the topmost spray of a sycamore sapling, was my wood warbler – only a little brown bird to be sure, but exquisitely delicate, with a pale yellow chest and throat.

I walked on up the hill pleased, feeling myself welcomed. I continued past the old stone church with its holy well, past an even older hut circle and past a squat standing stone older yet, to emerge on to the high plateau under Tal y Fan where wild ponies drifted like cloud shadow across the landscape. The sea glinted in the distance. The sky was filled with lark song and parachuting pipits. It was good to be back.

II
Further
AFIELD

Alone on a summit in the Silvretta.

14

Austria: Solo in the Silvretta

Ski touring is usually a sociable activity and among its many attractions is the camaraderie that can develop within a group. Numbers come in handy too in the event of injury, avalanche or crevasse rescue. However, I once found myself, towards the end of March, unexpectedly alone in Galtür in Austria. With the weather settled and the snowpack stable, it was not a difficult decision to head into the Silvretta Alps on my own. I even went so far as to leave behind my transceiver, shovel and probe, pieces of kit that ski tourers tend to feel naked without. I don't mind my own company and I relished the opportunity to be self-reliant for an extended period. The challenge would be avoiding the crowds as this is one of the most popular ski-touring areas in Europe. I am averse to crowds at the best of times but even more so in the mountains which, for me, are a refuge from the hurly-burly and sheer noisiness of the lowlands. So, seeking the way less travelled right from the start, I avoided the terrifyingly congested pistes of Ischgl and, instead, took the navette up valley to the small resort of Wirl.

Catching the earliest possible lifts, I was soon skimming across a frozen hillside away from the ski area and side-slipping between boulders and patches of heather into the deserted Vallüla valley. A few cautious turns on breakable crust and another long descending traverse brought me to a fork in the valley at 1,800 metres. Nursing a cold, I set off on the climb to the Bielerspitze at a sedate pace but by dint of pausing only to raise or lower heel lifts or to glance at the map tucked inside my shirt, I still gained height at a respectable 300 metres an hour. The familiar rhythm of skinning freed me to notice things other than the snow surface: the yellow green mottling of lichen on a protruding boulder, the murmur of a stream, the swish of gliding skins.

It was only just after midday when I reached the top, but it was not a moment too soon. The sun had been full on the steep south-facing slopes below for several hours already. Quickly I checked the map for the best line, and skied carefully down the west ridge until I could turn a band of small crags immediately beneath the summit. At first, all went well with the snow enjoyably soft to ski. However, as the angle steepened, the sun's rays were almost at a right angle to the slope and penetrating deep into the snowpack. The snow became correspondingly wetter and more dangerous. Now each turn was releasing snowballs that quickly grew to the size of lorry tyres which pursued me downhill, threatening to take me out. It added a new dimension to the phrase 'keep your eye on the ball'. But I was committed now and had no choice but to continue, slightly heart in mouth, hoping the whole slope did not slide away. I was not sorry to reach a shelf slanting down rightwards at an easier angle and in no time I was at the bottom. It never fails to astonish how quickly one loses height on skis, regardless of actual speed. A mere fifteen minutes after leaving the summit and 500 metres lower, I was stepping around deckchair sun-worshippers and their yapping dogs on to the terrace of the Gasthof Piz Buin. *Apfelstrudel* has never tasted so good.

I spent that night at the Madlenerhaus, a few hundred yards away amongst a collection of workmen's huts, under the wall of the Silvretta dam. It was all a bit of an anticlimax. The hut was an unprepossessing place, the welcome underwhelming and the food poor. At dinner I was given a table all to myself. On my own, English-speaking and a vegetarian, I felt like a leper. The only redeeming feature of my stay was a collection of photos of Ernest Hemingway on ski outside the hut in the 1920s.

Next day, as I langlaufed across the frozen lake, I was overtaken by a procession of noisy skidoos each towing up to a dozen skiers. Fortunately they were all heading up one valley for the large and very popular Wiesbadener hut whereas I was headed up another valley making for Switzerland where the huts are smaller, simpler and seemingly never crowded. Steep, awkward skinning up a slope much cut up by old ski tracks, with frequent kick-turns, led to a small glacier topped by the Schneeglocke at 3,223 metres. On the summit was a serious-looking group all dressed in uniform trousers and jackets, studying their maps intently. I took them to be Austrian aspirant guides being trained or tested for they looked at me slightly askance when I turned up on my own, but they soon turned back to their maps without saying anything. When they left a few minutes later, they looked to a man (and solitary woman) as if they had been born with skis on their feet. It was no surprise to find they had skied the whole of the steep, tight little chicane called the Roteflüh, no wider than a ski's length at times, down on to the Silvretta glacier. For me, discretion was the better part of valour and I downclimbed the bottom half on foot.

While the Austrians went up the glacier I went down it to reach the Silvretta hut where, in contrast to the previous night, the welcome could not have been warmer or friendlier. I was pleased to find that, despite a recent makeover, the panelled living room with its old, elaborately carved chairs and round tables embellished with beautiful marquetry was still the same. There were only a dozen people staying the night and someone was celebrating a fortieth birthday so it was a cheerful, convivial evening.

I was the only one up for an early breakfast the following morning. Skinning back up the silent, empty expanse of the Silvretta glacier, I felt very much alone, rather like the Ancient Mariner, except that I was glad to be there and savoured the feeling of solitude. Once over the briefly awkward Fuorcla dal Cunfin, however, I met the multitude coming up from the Wiesbadener hut and cramponed up and down Piz Buin in company, stepping over and under numerous ropes. Bottling out of the obvious challenge of the southeast couloir (forty degrees plus for 300 metres and still frozen hard at the top) I crossed a slightly higher but easier col back on to the Silvretta glacier and skied down to Plan Mezdi. Once again totally on my own, I could revel in thirty-five degree spring snow skiing right to the door of the virtually empty Tuoi hut and its three charming *gardiennes*.

The Wiesbadener hut next day back in Austria was packed as always with guided parties of every nationality but any curmudgeonly tendencies were dispelled by an evening in the company of a delightful German couple taking their first tentative steps into ski touring. I reached the hut over the straightforward Vermunt Pass, having first climbed the Piz de las Clavigliades by its north ridge. This was good value, up a steep crumbling snow arête with a couple of exciting off-balance moves with arms thrust in up to the shoulders to gain purchase. A short couloir descending direct from the ski depot looked as if it would be fun but proved to contain disappointingly crusted snow. No matter, it is part of the challenge of ski touring that all but the very best must constantly adapt, reducing speed or varying the radius of turn, as snow conditions change with altitude and aspect.

The following day saw me atop the fine spire of the Dreiländerspitze, with a sensationally exposed scramble to reach the true summit, before anyone else was about. Most people, it seems, climb it from the Jamtal hut, where breakfast is always half an hour later; travelling west to east has definite advantages. A traverse on foot across bare scree on the south side of the Vorderjamspitze followed to check out the Jamjoch, which is no longer an easy crossing of the watershed, thanks to glacial recession. Nowadays, the recommended route drops into a little basin south of the Hinter Jam Spitze. Meanwhile, low cloud had rolled in unexpectedly and flat light and a myriad of still-frozen ruts made for an unmemorable descent to the automatic sliding doors and impersonal efficiency of the busy Jamtal hut. These Austrian huts are not huts at all, but mountain hotels with hot showers, waitress service and rooms rather than dormitories which may explain why they seem to be always heaving when the Swiss huts, in this part of the world, are so quiet. The other factor, of course, is cost, Switzerland being undeniably more expensive than Austria, but personally I don't mind paying extra for virtually empty mountains.

On my final day I traversed the remote-feeling Schnapfenspitze, glad of *harscheisen* (ski crampons) for the steep hard-frozen initial slopes, taking great care with my kick-turns for a slip would have been impossible to check. Emerging into a secluded hanging valley, I half expected to see a herd of chamois but instead found cock snowfinches displaying and singing lustily from boulder tops. Spring was definitely in the air but a cold wind sprang up from nowhere and the plan for a leisurely break to enjoy the view from my last summit lost its appeal. Instead, it took only moments to strip the skins from my skis and head down the far side. The north-facing glacier soon became distinctly steep but the almost untracked snow, while not quite powder, was still soft even though it was weeks since the last snowfall. It was an exhilarating ski and at the bottom I could not resist pausing to admire my tracks, narcissistic though it felt. A short climb up to the Lareinfernerjoch led on to slopes of wet, collapsing snow from which bushes of heather and bilberry were beginning to emerge. It was horrible, leg-breaking stuff and having seen not a soul all day, it was without regret that I reached the large Heidelberger hut, a popular destination for day visitors brought up by skidoo or snow-cat. The slushy cat-track brought me eventually to an almost flat green piste leading into Ischgl where I took my only tumble of the week, observed with glee by a five-year-old and his mum whom I had overtaken moments earlier.

I had broken no records, achieved nothing of great significance, but it had been a wonderfully satisfying journey confirming my belief that it is always possible to get away from the crowds if you want to. Above all, being on my own had made it feel quite an adventure.

1 Looking down the gully on Yr Elen to Ffynnon Caseg.
2 Foel Fras in the Carneddau seen from the summit of Drum.
3 Glasgwm, Penmachno, home for over twenty years.
4 Looking towards Arenig Fawr from the Berwyns.
5 The Mawddach estuary near Barmouth at low tide.

6 Snowdon in winter seen from Capel Curig.
7 Jim Buckley running on Y Garn after work one evening, Snowdon behind.
8 The summit of Huandoy seen from Base Camp near the Paron glacier.

9 Looking west from the Silvretta range.
10 Bob Cole at the head of the Paron glacier.
11 Bob Cole in the Cordillera Blanca, Peru.

12 Mike Hendry skinning through the cedars of Lebanon.
13 Geoff Cohen and Des Rubens after a bivouac on the summit ridge
   of Delusion Peak (6,500 metres) in the Kishtwar Himal.

14 Skiing down Kedar Dome (6,830 metres), Gangotri.
15 Robert Sykes and Neil Laing at the high camp on Kedar Dome.
16 Des Rubens in Zanskar.
17 Geoff Cohen in Zanskar.

18 The author at 7,000 metres on Annapurna IV.   *Photo: Dick Isherwood.*
19 Heading for the top of Delusion Peak in a brief clearing, bivouac site in the background.
20 Dick Isherwood at a high camp during the attempt on Annapurna II.
21 Gyatso, a Zanskari pony man, reciting his prayers at a lunch stop.
22 Nepali girls in the Marsyandi valley.

23 Fences in the uplands, a bone of contention.
24 Skiers on the Haute Route.
25 The Bertol hut, a staging post on the Haute Route.
26 Alpine ski touring. Peter Cliff and other British guides on a training course near Chamonix.

25

26

27

28

27 Twin Otters at Patriot Hills.
28 Uphill skinning on a ski tour in the Alps.

Soloing the lower section of the Gletscherhorn North Face above Lauterbrunnen.
Photo: Rob Ferguson.

15

Switzerland: Gletscherhorn North Face

It had been raining for a week, they told us when we arrived in Lauter-brunnen. It drizzled steadily most of the way up to the Rottal hut. At two o'clock next morning the mist was still down and we spent a cheerless day in the cold empty hut, nibbling dry bread and eyeing bundles of wood at an unaffordable price. Every now and then the mist would lift a little to reveal the rocky lower face. Very impressive it was too, but the notorious séracs remained out of sight hanging somewhere above. By this time, however, we did not really believe that we were going to climb the mountain, it was just a matter of propitiating conscience. We were not in the least surprised when at two o'clock the second morning the mist was at exactly the same level, less than half way up the face. Purely as a formality we reset the alarm for three thirty and it was without interest that we poked our heads out of the window when it went off again. But, lo and behold, this time the moon was shining bright, and there was the face, all 1,200 metres of it, looking huge and dark and magnificent, only a wisp of cloud hovering in front of the rocks and the séracs bristling and gleaming up above, but apparently to one side of our line. I was almost angry. It couldn't be true, it was just a trick to get us out of bed. Still suspicious, we stuffed ourselves with muesli and more bread and it was not until we were crossing the glacier, with the sun just over the edge of the world and head torches unnecessary, that scepticism was replaced by enthusiasm.

The slope below the bergschrund was like dough, soggy and unfrozen. The bridges over the bergschrund were soft too, so we kept falling through till we found the right way. But these were little things when day was coming to a sky miraculously clear, even if there was a lowering bank of cloud on the horizon. The climbing was interesting from the start, Scottish II and III with easier ground between. There is no point using a rope unless it is needed, so we picked our own lines. I followed a shallow couloir, which contained some little bulges, but the ice was perfect and axe and hammer picks bit in reassuringly. Rob took to the rocks on the right, which was out of character, but then he is always suspicious of couloirs. After a couple of hundred metres my ice became a bit too steep and I traversed across to join Rob. The rock rib had petered out and he was on steep mixed ground, ice with helpful rock handholds. A little higher, Rob became involved with some unfriendly slabs so I went off further to the right which was awkward also – delicate moves on thin ice.

Above was the big rock barrier that splits the face horizontally. The only way through looked to be an intimidating ice pitch. From a distance it had seemed a gully, but in fact it was more of an icefall. There seemed to be no alternative, however, so I climbed the slope beneath it and then broke left up a steep little chimney to bypass as much as possible, until I was beneath a vertical rock wall. I took a belay and dropped Rob an end of the rope. He took a traverse line to the right about five metres lower, on snowed-up rock. '*Fifty Nine Face*' route must be like this', he mused (referring to the winter climb on Creag Meagaidh), as he peeled away chunks of ice to excavate rock holds. It looked rather too steep for comfort and I think we both perked up when a moac nestled into a tailor-made slot. A funny move with a knee and then Rob was on a snowy ramp leading rightwards on to the upper section of the ice pitch. Behind the startling red of his helmet and cagoule, the sky was blue and the sunlight was just beginning to creep across the séracs. Down below, the face was visible as a series of broad snow ledges up which our footprints wandered, reappearing slightly offset at the top of invisible steps. People look for different things in their climbing, but this was how I wanted it. We were on our own, committed, with no one above to drop a top rope and no one below to call the helicopter. There aren't many places left in the Alps where that's true.

'Only forty foot to go', shouted Rob. 'Looks steep, though,' he added as an afterthought. Then he moved out of sight round the corner and I could see and hear no more. I expected the climbing to be hard but that rope moved slowly by any standards. The snow may not have frozen lower down, but up here it felt quite cold enough. My Dachstein mitts were petrified into solid lumps and my feet felt the same way. Streams of spindrift were flowing down the face all around and every so often, one of them found a way over the rock barrier and down my neck. Longingly I watched the sunlight across the face, so near yet two hours away at least. I thought of the pile jacket in my sack, but always it seemed that Rob must be nearly there and I did not bother. Instead I jumped up and down in my steps and banged my hands together, though it did not feel safe doing both at once. My right leg was shaking uncontrollably. Then, for no particular reason, it stopped and the left one started. I gibbered quietly to myself and occasionally yelled wordlessly into space, which seemed to have a slight warming effect. A few feet of rope moved out. A faint voice shouted that it had a nut runner and was nearly there. Life suddenly seemed more cheerful. Then nothing happened for almost half an hour. The rope never moved. There wasn't even the encouraging sound of chipping and I relapsed into numbed apathy.

When eventually the rope leaped out and Rob yelled that he had an axe belay, it took a while to re-coordinate mind and body and the first few moves were desperate. Clumsy frozen mitts could not grip the holds and when a projecting rock gave way beneath my feet I nearly fell off, crampon points scratching frantically till they caught on something. But, as usual, it didn't take long to warm up and soon I was stepping round on to the ice that had taken Rob such an age. I could see why. It was not simply that it was steep, though many of the moves were out of balance, but the ice was rotten, inspiring no confidence, and in places very thin so that our new-fangled tools were of no help. Being an icefall rather than a gully and having half the face stretched below, the exposure was unnerving. It was a fine piece of climbing, which would have been Grade V on Ben Nevis.

We knew we'd cracked it after that. The top half of the face consists of fairly steep slopes, about fifty-five degrees, but unless the ice turned really nasty we did not expect any problems. And in fact it was beautiful soft ice most of the way, the sort on which you feel you are front-pointing but really the first down points are biting as well. In places unstable flour had accumulated in runnels which wasn't too pleasant because at that angle you never know what is making it stick. Sometimes the really hard permanent stuff came a little too close to the surface for peace of mind. But neither lasted long enough to prevent us moving together. I was in front, climbing fast, glad just to be warm again and revelling in the sense of space and isolation induced by the sweep of ice above, below and on either hand; but Rob had a bad cold which was slowing him down. Earlier, following his steps, I had kept finding these green things on the ice. Now, as we zigzagged through rock outcrops and round bulges, our progress was interrupted by volleys of retching coughs. I was impressed by the way Rob managed to keep going. The Rottalhorn col was well below by this time, the summit rocks looked close. The slope steepened for a last fling and the ice became harder. In went a drive-in ice screw and I kept moving. A brief pause fifty metres later while Rob took it out and I was on the corniced saddle just below the summit being welcomed by a bitter wind.

As we chewed dried bananas in the lee of some rocks, we felt pleased with ourselves at being up so quickly. But congratulations were premature. Suddenly the Jungfrau disappeared and a grumbling and a rumbling came from the distance. Luckily the storm centre remained over the Aletschhorn but the descent was fairly wild all the same, groping through near whiteout among angry whirling snow devils. On the flat col of the Kranzberg I jumped across a crevasse, not realising it was on the rim of a slope. I landed flat on my face, winded and wondering for a moment how I had reached the bottom of the hole so quickly. Nor was the route as simple as the photo in the book implied – descents never are – huge rifts splitting what should have been a gentle snow slope.

It was good to reach the furrow winding up to the Jungfraujoch and the Tolkienesque little door tucked away at the base of a cliff, where you would never notice it but for the track. The last train was on the point of leaving. The gnome in the ticket office wasn't pleased at being recalled and he was even less pleased when we paid him with an assortment of Swiss, French and English currency. Kleine Scheidegg was wrapped in mist, which turned to a fine drizzle as we arrived. This was where we came in. Wistfully we watched the tourists trooping off to the big hotel and the solid Swiss railwaymen tucked behind their beers in the brightly lit station buffet. But we had no money left and the prospect of a bivouac, even at Kleine Scheidegg, did not appeal. We headed downwards into the gloom.

We had not gone far before virtue was rewarded by a slight clearing of the sky and traces of pink in the west. The evening was warm and still and the tranquillity of the landscape with its cowbells, orchids and waterfalls, contrasted sharply with the elemental hostility of two hours earlier. It was like one of those huge sombre nineteenth-century paintings, except that it did not feel at all gloomy. Rather, it reminded me of the quiet bit after the storm in Beethoven's Pastoral Symphony. At Wengen, the first fireworks were being let off into the dusk and groups of children were gathering with coloured lanterns. We remembered that it was August 1st, the Swiss national holiday. Two years before, to the day, folk watching the fireworks down in the valley had seen our head torches on top of the Grosshorn. As we descended the steep muddy track to Lauterbrunnen, bonfires flared below and a band struck up, making us feel like conquering heroes being welcomed home. Except that no one would give us a lift the last four miles up the road to the campsite. Fortunately, we were too tired and too content to care. Next day it was raining properly.

Artesonraju seen from a sheltered camp among some trees.

16

Peru: Summer Break in the Blanca

The central locking system of the taxi gave a sudden clunk. 'Naughty people here', said the driver cryptically. Bob and I looked at each other. We were stationary at a red traffic light on a broad, not particularly busy street in downtown Lima. Friends had warned us about Lima. One had had a necklace torn from her throat; another had his watch cut from his wrist. But we had assumed we were safe enough in a taxi. Speaking no Spanish in a country where few people speak English, we were very much innocents abroad. The driver was clearly concerned and watched over us until we had bought our bus tickets to Huaraz and seen our kitbags and rucksacks safely stowed at the back of the office. We were grateful.

Bob had wanted an adventure. I had always wanted to climb in Peru, so we joined forces. June to August is winter in the southern hemisphere, but it is also the dry season in the Andes and the best for climbing.

77

We opted to go in late June. Bob bought the tickets; I bought and borrowed maps and guides and tried to decide where to go. Initially, we wanted to climb somewhere remote but we soon realised that with only three weeks we might have to settle for somewhere more accessible. The Cordillera Blanca is the place, we were told, if you want easy access and short walk-ins, plus stable weather. Although Netti had given me a Spanish phrasebook for my birthday, somehow I never got round to studying it. Perhaps my abysmal track record with both French and Welsh had something to do with it. We arrived in Lima with not a word of Spanish between us, apart from *buenas días* and *gracias*. The problem was solved when we booked, by chance, into a hotel in Huaraz that is also a trekking agency. The Swiss manageress spoke good English and made all our travel arrangements for us. Admittedly, it was at a price but that side of things went like clockwork.

However, where or what should we climb in the Blanca? Although it is only one of Peru's four major climbing areas (the other being the Cordillera Huayhuash, Vilacamba and Vilcanota) it is still an immensely long chain sub-divided into many different mountain groups. Of course, we had heard of famous peaks like Alpamayo, 'the world's most beautiful mountain', and Huascaran, the highest peak in Peru. But, by the same token, everybody wants to climb them and we heard tales of crowded camps, fixed ropes, in-situ anchors and queues in descent. It all sounded rather like so many alpine routes that have become trivialised by their popularity. Although mountaineering has become, of necessity, a social activity, being old-fashioned I still object to climbing in a crocodile and I rather enjoy making my own tracks and using my own judgement. So I was still scratching my head over an objective when I bumped into Martin Doyle at Plas y Brenin. He thought for a moment and then said, 'There is a peak called Artisan something or other that is supposed to be really good.' Bob and I looked at the guidebook and discovered that Artesonraju is 6,025 metres high with a south-east face graded Difficile. We looked at the map and saw that the Paron valley is a dead end so no trekking routes run through it, and we decided it would do us just fine for a first foray.

Huaraz is at 3,000 metres and there is noticeably less oxygen available to the body. We spent two slightly breathless days there, buying food and fuel for ten days and allowing ourselves to adapt before heading into the mountains. In a hired Jeep with three porters, one of whom was to stay on as a camp-minder, we descended nearly a thousand metres on the main road to Caraz. Then the driver engaged four-wheel drive for the steep, rough track ahead. At first the road wound through small fields edged with cactus, broom in exuberant yellow flower and gum trees coppiced for firewood and timber, not to mention a hundred ferns, flowers and shrubs unknown to us. A wide variety of crops and vegetables were being grown, women in brightly coloured clothes and straw hats doing most of the work, it seemed. Homesteads with neat mud-bricked walls and tiled roofs were dotted about the hillside, often with pigs tethered outside. Then, abruptly, cultivation was left behind as the road swung left to enter a narrow canyon filled with scrub forest, switch-backing madly to gain height at the very foot of huge granite cliffs. Finally the angle eased and, three hours after leaving Huaraz, we arrived at the dam wall of Lago Paron, a startlingly green glacial lake surrounded by snowy peaks, their tops wrapped in storm cloud. The altitude was almost 4,200 metres.

Twenty minutes after arriving the porters had sorted out their loads, we had signed a book for somebody in a uniform, and we were on our way through thickets of sweet-smelling blue lupins along the north shore of the lake. Two hours later, after some easy walking and a leisurely lunch, we were startled to find ourselves at what was apparently Base Camp, according to the porters. We were not impressed. It was obviously a well-used spot and there were some other tents pitched already. On the other hand, it was windy, a herd of cattle was wandering around, the sun had already disappeared for the duration behind some high crags, and we had gained no height since leaving the vehicle. A recce revealed a flat if wind-swept site by the little Lago Artesoncocha, half an hour's walk further up the valley and a hundred metres higher. As we were paying the porters for two days' work we felt no compunction about calling the shots. Reluctantly they hoisted their loads on to their backs. 'Loco', muttered Darwin, our saturnine camp 'guardian'. We pretended not to understand.

The following day two of the porters departed leaving the lugubrious Darwin all alone in an enormous tent, while we followed a well-used path up a moraine crest to a point from which one could descend easily enough over boulders on to the glacier. There we found a number of tent platforms and bivvy sites and a lone Spaniard with a tummy-bug. From time to time we could see his two mates struggling with a bergschrund on Paron Grande, 5,600 metres, up in the cloud at the head of the valley.

His knowledge of English matched ours of Spanish but as we left, in an unexpected gesture, he handed us a bag of coca leaves. We chewed them dutifully with no discernible effect and eventually passed them on to Darwin, which at least raised a smile. More exciting were glimpses of Artesonraju, a dramatic pyramid of snow and ice at the sight of which Bob went very quiet. Bob is no tyro, having climbed Mont Blanc and the Frendo Spur for a start, but face climbs were something new. They are never as steep and gnarly as they look, I told him, almost convincing myself. Bob said nothing.

On the way down I spotted a possible campsite among a grove of trees (they had a curious, flaky, orange bark and, we learned later, were called quenual). Investigation revealed that it was an idyllic spot with a stream of clear water running through it and almost completely sheltered from the cold, ever-present wind that seemed to characterise the valley. At 4,550 metres it was also that little bit higher and better for acclimatization, so in two carries we upped sticks and moved camp that afternoon. Even Darwin approved when he discovered that it was not only calm and quiet, but did not lose the sun until six in the evening.

Over the next few days we learned a great deal about the mountain environment in which we found ourselves. A walk up to 5,000 metres beneath the Caraz group of peaks revealed that, like so many mountains in this part of the world, hanging ice of one description or another, be it huge cornices, active séracs or chaotic icefalls, ensures that attractive lines are few and far between. A bivvy at the top of the moraine emphasized that nights on the equator are long – the sun sets at around six and rises again twelve hours later, with sitting around over a brew not really an option thanks to the wind. We made an unsuccessful attempt on Paron Grande, learning that the glacier was smothered in deep, unconsolidated snow that made movement of any sort desperately hard work. But we did, finally, discover a way over the bergschrund that enabled us to return a day later and climb the peak, starting and finishing in the dark. Almost throughout, the snow was bottomless sugar (facetted grains and depth hoar because the face receives virtually no sun) varying from forty-five degrees to fifty-five degrees. It was hard graft, creating a trench with the knee first, before deepening it with the foot, but somehow the slope was more stable than one would have expected. It didn't slide, anyway. We learned that a snow stake buried horizontally, and strengthened by axe and hammer placed vertically in front of it at each end, was the only remotely worthwhile form of belay. And crossing a bergschrund near the top showed us, if we needed showing, that heel hooking in big boots and crampons at 5,500 metres makes you puff. It was all very instructive. It was just a shame that the cloud rolled in as we reached the summit ridge so we saw nothing at all the other side.

Now it was time to have a stab at Artesonraju. Stunning to look at, with no objective danger to speak of, it seemed to be a peak that many aspired to but relatively few actually climbed. During our ten-day stay several different groups toiled up the moraine to camp at the top or on the glacier but only three teams actually made it to the summit. It may have been the weather that deterred the others, for it was far from perfect. It may have been the deep snow. Or it may simply have been the appearance of the face, because it certainly was impressive, and only made more intimidating by the sight of a couple of tiny dots slowly, slowly progressing up or down. Be that as it may, appearances are often deceptive and there is only one way to find out what a climb is really like.

'Time spent in reconnaissance is seldom wasted.' Never was there a truer saying, particularly in mountaineering. We broke camp after a leisurely breakfast and repitched the trusty Quasar on the glacier beneath the face at about 4,900 metres. This gave us time to check out the route to the bergschrund 300 metres higher. We were glad that we did so as there were a number of large, poorly bridged crevasses and finding a way through them in the dark would not have been easy. Somebody had marked a route with bamboo wands but bridges had collapsed since then and they were more of a hindrance than a help until we repositioned them. However, the bergschrund itself was easy to cross and the slope above, initially at least, was no more than forty-five degrees. We returned to the tent feeling confident.

The alarm went off at two o'clock. The wind had been whipping snow against the tent noisily and ominously but when we looked out, fearing the worst, it was to find a perfect night, lit by a full moon. Torches were totally redundant as we plodded up the first slopes and threaded and jumped our way through the crevasse zone, the rope tight between us. On the face, the snow was the usual deep sugar except when there were traces of old tracks where it had firmed up a little. We pitched it from the start, as much to give ourselves a breather as for security. As we climbed, the huge bright moon was sinking on our left even as the sun began to strain at the horizon on our right.

I was well up the fourth pitch, kicking steps in slightly firmer snow for once and thinking how lucky we were to have such a perfect day for the climb, when I glanced across to find the summit of Paron Grande obscured by cloud and the sky almost completely covered. From then on we saw very little. After ten fifty-metre run-outs we paused for a bite to eat and put away the head torches. From time to time we could see the top, looking quite close, thanks to foreshortening, but the altimeter told us we were at 5,650 metres, just over halfway up.

Now the slope began to steepen, the snow grew deeper and more sugary and the weather closed in. The summit disappeared and clouds of spin-drift were blowing across the face. Wind, cloud, snow became the limits of our little world. I was wearing a pair of new, lightweight plastic boots, Scarpa Alphas, which were unproven in cold conditions. I was concerned when my toes began to feel cold and then went numb, delighted when they began to hurt. Bob's toes, in traditional plastic boots, remained numb for days afterwards so I reckon my boots passed the test.

The last two pitches were up runnels between flutings, at least sixty degrees and only made more awkward and insecure by old steps which had created bulges. Finally, the angle eased and we emerged on to the summit ridge where someone had left a bamboo wand. It felt like the top but it was not the true summit. A line of old steps, filled in but still visible, led up the gently angled ridge into the mist – how far was anyone's guess. Large flakes of snow had begun to fall and it suddenly felt a rather lonely place. 'What do you think, Bob?' I asked, indicating the steps, 'I'm not sure if it's worth it.' Bob had slowed down over the last few pitches and now, at 6,000 metres, was looking ashen. 'I'm not bothered, mate', he replied.

There are no easy ways off in this part of the world, so it was back the way we had come. The top two pitches we abseiled from bollards, leaving behind sections of a cardboard box as a low-tech, biodegradable solution to the problem of the rope slicing through the snow. Then it was endless downclimbing, pitch after pitch, our uphill trench obliterated already by spindrift and new snow. Once, a powder avalanche poured down on top of us. It was alarming, but also reassuring to know that the new snow was sliding off rather than building up to more dangerous depths. As the afternoon wore on, the temperature began to drop again, beards clotted, gloves froze solid. We never did discover a good way of carrying the snow stakes, short of taking a pack off, and a right pain they were too. Near the bottom, going through some rocks, we discovered a couple of old anchors but by the time we had uncoiled the second rope and set up an abseil, it was no quicker than continuing to downclimb. The light was fading as we picked a cautious way through the crevasses, all traces of our morning's track gone. It would be a bad time to dangle in space. We reached the tent fifteen hours after leaving it, just as the sky cleared and the summit reappeared far above. We slept the sleep of the just that night.

By the time we had returned to Huaraz for a shower and a change from pasta, we only had four days left to play with. Fit and acclimatised now, we employed Shanks' pony instead of porters and in an energetic push, found ourselves attempting an unclimbed ridge on a 6,000-metre peak with neither sight nor sound of other climbers anywhere. But that is another story.

Robert Sykes, Tracker and Neil Laing on the lower slopes of Kedar Dome, Shivling behind.

17

India: Kedar Dome on Skis

Eyes closed, I recline against a slab of granite, warmed by the sun. Mainly I am conscious of sounds, the distant roar of a glacial river, the chirruping of orange-billed choughs, the sighing of wind in the grass just above my sheltered hollow, the buzz of a fly close to my ear. It is very peaceful and I feel utterly relaxed after the exertions of the last few days.

Opening my eyes, the broad plain of Tapovan, which translates as 'place of meditation', is a study in greys and browns. At the tail end of winter, the snow has gone but the grass has not yet begun to grow. Enclosed on two sides by moraine walls a hundred metres high, it is dominated on the third by the magnificent up-thrust of rock and ice which forms one of the world's great mountains – Shivling, or Shiva's Lingam. Specks of vivid colour in the landscape reveal the presence of two very different cultures to each of which this is a special place. Most prominent are the climbers' encampments, the yellow, blue and purple tents of three small expeditions from France, Switzerland and Germany, attempting routes on Shivling and the Bhagirathi peaks. Less obvious but equally distinctive are yellow and red flags fluttering from poles dotted about the hillsides and the saffron robes of sadhus sitting cross-legged or squatting on their haunches outside stone-walled shelters. For some this is the end of a long journey on foot from the plains of India, although it must be said that most use public transport where it is available. They follow the sacred river Ganges up to the ancient temple at Gangotri and on to the Cow's Mouth at Gaumukh, where the Bhagirathi river, one of the sources of Mother Ganga, flows from the glacier's snout. For most pilgrims, and this includes throngs of ordinary Indians, not just holy men, this is far enough. They bathe briefly in the river and sip its water, and return with aching heads to lower altitudes. Every year a few venture too near and are killed when blocks of ice break away suddenly or boulders slide down on top of them. A few pilgrims, however, leave Gaumukh below and press on over the jumbled rocks and dirty ice of the glacier and up a final steep moraine to arrive at Tapovan, an oasis of tranquillity in a restless, elemental mountain world.

A group of us from the Eagle Ski Club are camped out of sight at the other end of Tapovan. We hope to make a ski ascent of Kedar Dome (6,831 metres), but our first attempt on the summit has ground to a halt in a metre of exhausting and potentially dangerous new snow, and the four of us in the 'A' Team have returned to Base Camp to recuperate. As its name suggests, the snowy northern slopes of the mountain are at an ideal angle for skiing, mostly twenty to thirty degrees with the odd steeper section, but it is heavily glaciated. Sérac walls and bands of large crevasses ensure that one cannot roam at will but must weave about to find and follow the best line. The peak is out of sight from Tapovan. The base of it, where we have left our skis and ski boots, is a full day's journey away. At first the walking is delightful, over grass and stable scree. A detour on to the Gangotri glacier to avoid some cliffs is less pleasant, a prolonged balancing act over unstable boulders; then a moraine crest leads to a grassy ablation valley where wild goats browse beneath the towering crags. Finally, the route crosses the Khati Barak side glacier, every day's melt under the hot May sun stripping away more of the snow to reveal bare ice embedded with stones. There, at the foot of Kedar Dome at 4,800 metres we can at last use our skis. It is a journey we come to know well during our three-week stay. It is not always pleasurable, especially at first. Shoulders ache and chests heave, prompting muttering in the ranks about high-altitude porters, or rather the lack of them. At least the process makes us fitter and stronger and allows us to acclimatise.

Things become harder above the snow line where the heat of the high May sun and the glare of light reflected off the snow are unbelievably enervating. 'Glacier lassitude' the old-timers used to call it. White shirts and white sun hats help but even by nine in the morning it is becoming noticeable, so early starts are *de rigeur*. Usually, we find ourselves pitching camp or dumping loads by midday, unable to take anymore, leaving the afternoons to melt snow for endless cups of tea.

But it is not all a summit-oriented slog. There are moments of startling beauty, especially in the cool light of dawn and dusk. The snowfields of Kedar Dome glowing pink far above us, or Shivling from a high camp, twin-headed from this angle, like some gigantic fish diving into a sea of boiling cloud, prompt me to think only of the privilege of being there. There are moments of intimacy when tent companions reminisce about home, disclose some of their hopes and fears, or merely fantasise about food. And then there is the skiing. The reward for several ascents from 4,800 to 5,800 metres is a wonderful spring-snow descent every time, an effortless swoop back down the slopes we have just toiled up so painfully. Almost as enjoyable is the sight of Nick Parks tightly linking his telemark turns, a broad grin splitting his bearded, sunburned face.

In the Himalaya, what ultimately decides success or failure is not skill, determination or equipment, but the weather, and so far we have been blessed with near-perfect conditions. Only on a couple of nights have we been kept awake by the rattling and shaking of the tent in strong winds interspersed by ominous silences which mean not that the weather has improved, but that we are being quietly buried by snow. Unfortunately, this one break in the weather precedes our summit attempt and we retreat from 6,300 metres, sinking in up to our thighs as soon as we unwisely step off our skis. Leaving the tents at 5,800 metres for the next team, led by Nick, to use on their attempt, we descend to Base Camp to lick our wounds and gird up our loins for a second go.

In the event, the others are unsuccessful too, and when we head back up the mountain, there are only three of us. Neil Laing, keen, lean and in his late twenties, taking most things in his stride, uphill and down; Robert Sykes, a pensioner who claims that it is his garden in the Lake District that keeps him so extraordinarily fit; and myself, leader and instigator of the trip which is commemorating the seventy-fifth anniversary of the Eagle Ski Club. Acclimatised and familiar with the route, we travel from Base Camp to our top camp in a day. Above, the snow has settled and consolidated in our absence, but to be on the safe side we move up next day and pitch a tent under a small sérac at 6,400 metres. We are gambling that the weather will hold and that evening we watch anxiously as swirling cloud fills the valleys below. But we are in luck and it comes to nothing.

Three squeezed into a tent designed for two may sound cosy, but it does not make for a comfortable night and we have rehydrated too well for our own good. Before dawn we are all awake and keen to be moving. We brew up, force down some muesli and crawl outside into the starlit night. It is bitterly cold and beards quickly clot with ice. Cramming inner boots into stiff plastic shells is even more of a struggle than usual. Putting on harnesses, tying on to the rope and fitting skins to skis we fumble in warm but bulky over-mitts, not needed up to now, and it is light by the time we are ready. Once moving, we gain height steadily and soon we meet the sun, which casts our shadows hugely across the snow. Skirting a band of crevasses and sometimes zigzagging tightly to avoid areas where wind-slab has accumulated, we arrive on a ridge where the snow has been hardened and eroded by wind into sastrugi, breaking waves and free-standing plinths of snow, horrible to ski, even uphill. Pausing briefly to fit *harscheisen* (ski crampons) to our skis, we find ourselves, much sooner than expected and less than two hours after leaving the tent, on the summit of Kedar Dome. It has all been straightforward and might almost be an anticlimax. But it isn't. The wonderful clarity of the early-morning light and the countless peaks of Garhwal and Tibet protruding from a sea of cloud make sure of that. Nevertheless, it is too cold for contemplation. We gaze around, only half-believing that we are really there, but saving congratulations for later when we are safely off the mountain. Then we strip skins from our skis and point them downhill for the long, long descent to Base Camp. Fresh food, hot water, spring flowers and lazy contentment await. But first, there is 2,000 metres of skiing to savour …

Two days later Nick, with Steve Gould, Steve Wright and Jamie Howard, also reaches the summit and we clear the mountain of our equipment. In less than a week we are back home.

Syrian army observation post on a summit in the Lebanon.

18

Lebanon: A Ski Tour in the Lebanon

'I can't believe we're doing this,' said Roger, plaintively. It was a clear but moonless night, dark enough – I had noticed a few minutes earlier – for Venus to cast a thin ray of light across the flat, frozen surface of the snow. Now we were edging tentatively on skis across a rapidly steepening slope, the limited beam from a Petzl Mini head torch doing little to reassure us. I said nothing. The slope felt exposed and scary but from the movement of the other torches fifty yards ahead I could tell that this was, in fact, no more than a hollow in the undulating plateau. Roger, however, was tired and cross and feared the worst. We came to a point where the others had side-stepped but it seemed simpler to take the skis off and kick steps for a few feet to the top of the slope. We were greeted by an icy wind that chilled us as soon as we stopped moving. Below were the friendly lights of villages. They looked deceptively close, but we knew that not only were they several miles away but that between us and them, the ground dropped precipitously for six hundred metres. Skins attached to the undersides of our touring skis, we were following the rim of the plateau seeking the descent route through the cliffs that our local guide knew from the summer. It had been a long day and it was not over yet.

The six of us from the Eagle Ski Club were on the second day of a traverse of the Lebanon range. It had sounded an unlikely destination for a ski holiday when Mike and Valerie first suggested it but Roger had lived there in the sixties and spoke enthusiastically of skiing in the morning and swimming in the Mediterranean in the afternoon. Local sources assured us that the civil war was a thing of the past and that visitors were welcome and even the Foreign Office said that there should be no danger, provided we kept away from the border with Israel in the south. Our informants were right on all counts. Although there are still plenty of bomb craters and pock-marked buildings, it is ten years since the war ended and Lebanon is well on the road to recovery after the seventeen years of turmoil that blighted it in the seventies and eighties. Everywhere, people were warm and welcoming and, it turns out, the country has a thriving little ski industry. There are half a dozen small resorts, and while none are bigger than Cairngorm or Aonach Mòr, the snow seems to be considerably more reliable than Scotland. Every weekend Lebanese skiers pour out of Beirut and up into the mountains to have fun on the pistes. The market is big enough for Rossignol to have sent over a demonstration team of young French and American hotshots whom we met during our stay.

After a warm-up day on and off piste at Zaarour, only thirty-five kilometres from Beirut, we set off for Faraya, Lebanon's biggest and busiest ski resort. Initially the country was rolling, with thorn bushes and small outcrops of limestone poking through a thin snow cover. The views were spectacular, down steep but populated hillsides on to the Mediterranean, and inland to the snow-covered hills of the Anti-Lebanon range on the Syrian border in the east, and the snowy bulk of Mount Harmon to the south. Here we encountered the only other ski tourers we were to meet in Lebanon, a group of French ex-pats, living in Beirut. A more sustained climb, zigzagging up a steep ridge brought us to the summit of Jabal Sannine, 2,620 metres, where we were greeted by friendly boy soldiers in flip-flops from a Syrian army observation post. The Syrians, we learned later, had been invited to restore law and order at the end of the civil war, but now seem to have outstayed their welcome. A broad rolling plateau, like snow-covered sand dunes – though actually limestone – brought us, as the sun was setting, to the deserted pistes of Faraya and the welcome comforts of the Auberge Suisse.

We had always known that day two of the traverse was going to be a big one. In fact, our original plan had involved a camp or bivvy, but we were more than happy to travel light when we learned it was possible in a day. However, route finding was going to be complex and we were advised to take a guide. Aram was a good looking gentle giant, the offspring of an Armenian father and a Danish mother, with a French as well as a Lebanese passport. He had just completed his National Service in France, mostly spent on ski by the sound of it, and was about to start a degree in Business Studies at Beirut University. He was a delightful man, but so formidably fit that our usual view of him was a speck on the horizon.

We left Faraya early in the morning and for an hour and a half skinned along a flat road, its surface packed hard by countless skidoos. Every so often a group of machines would roar past, the local lads taking their molls for a spin. The sun shone in a cloudless sky and our feet were becoming hot and sore. It gradually dawned on us that the route we were taking might be suitable for Nordic skiers but it was not going to be much fun on our heavier alpine equipment, nor was there much prospect of any skiing. Impatiently, we decided to abandon the long contouring, horse-shoe-shaped route that was familiar to Aram in favour of a more direct line involving some major ups and downs. The only problem was the map. Actually, we had two – a 1:1 million road map of the whole of Lebanon and an enlargement of a map taken off the internet at a scale of about 1:150,000 – we were not exactly sure – with a contour interval of 100 metres. To all intents and purposes, we would have to follow our noses.

It certainly proved a more interesting route. We soon left the skidoos behind and were rewarded by some superb descents, swooping down through scattered juniper bushes on perfect spring snow, as well as the inevitable long climbs that followed them. Aram was at pains to allay any fears we might have. Parts of the countryside are still littered with land-mines but, he assured us, they are not a problem in winter. Provided they are covered by thirty centimetres of snow they will not detonate. Once, we heard artillery and machine-gun fire in the distance. Just local hunters, we were told ... We were not moving fast and, as the day wore on, it became apparent that we were not going to reach our destination. At first, we were not too perturbed. There was a major valley not far ahead and it seemed a simple matter to drop down into it, descend to the nearest village and telephone for a taxi.

This decision made, all went well for a while, even though the valley was much further away than we had realised and we were moving very slowly by now. As the sun dropped and with it the temperature – instantly creating a breakable crust – we skied carefully down, thinking we had timed it perfectly. And then Aram suddenly stopped, looking helpless. We were on a convex slope, dropping into a deep gorge. The streambed we had been following was a line of weakness cutting the wall of the gorge but it was becoming steep and a hundred metres below it disappeared completely. From what we could see of the opposite wall and from what we knew of limestone country in general, it was almost certainly leading us to a vertical impasse. The realisation slowly dawned that our safest way out was not down. Visions of beer and bath receded into the distant future. Wearily we put skins back on to our skis and retraced our tracks back up the hill, not quite sure what to do next. We could always bivvy for the night in the group shelter someone suggested. My reply was, I am sorry to say, unprintable. Unplanned bivouacs are not my idea of fun.

By the time we reached the cairn from where we had started the descent, it was dark and we stopped to rummage for head torches. At this opportune moment our crestfallen guide (though the situation was more of our making than his) came up with Plan B and the technology to back it up, namely a mobile phone that worked and a father with a four-wheel drive vehicle who would meet us as high up a rough mountain track as he could get. All we had to do was follow the plateau rim southwards to find the point where the summer track emerged from below. It sounded simple. But the road would be covered in snow and invisible on the plateau in daylight, let alone at night. And would Aram recognise the spot? He assured us he knew it well. But as the minutes lengthened into an hour and then an hour and a half and we were still on the plateau, skins whirring like dynamos when we skied down, tired legs and blistered feet complaining when we trudged up, even the most optimistic began to wonder. Roger was a resilient sixty-eight but he had been flagging for some time. Now his pace was faltering, his rests becoming longer and more frequent.

Then, quite suddenly, we were descending into a defile, a distinct geo-graphical feature marked by a large juniper tree. Shortly afterwards, wonder of wonders, we could discern the outline of a track winding its way encouragingly downwards. In the dark, it was safer to keep skins on rather than try to ski the narrow track, but all the same we lost height rapidly and with relief until the snow ran out. Skis were strapped on to the sides of packs and tied at the tips, A-frame style, and we continued on down. We caught a glimpse of some headlights not so very far below. And then came the sting in the tail. Just when thoughts of food and beer were beginning to resurface, the track infuriatingly began to contour the mountainside. For over a kilometer it lost no height at all, and in places snow had drifted deeply. From time to time, tantalisingly, we could see the interior light of the vehicle down below but it was getting no closer. Somewhere ahead the advance guard – Aram, with Mike and Derek – was breaking trail. In the rear, Valerie and Jay were encouraging an exhausted Roger. In between, I plodded along feeling that the day had definitely gone on long enough, the weight of Roger's skis as well as my own pulling my small pack uncomfortably backwards. But all things come to an end and eventually the track dived abruptly downwards, twisting and turning stonily until, where it levelled out unexpectedly, we reached the parked Range Rover. A kilometre further down was a second vehicle. A shuttle was needed to get all of us down to the lower point, and then half an hour's drive through the dark, climbing steadily back up to the snow line again, brought us finally to a hotel at the tiny resort of Laqlouq, where the staff valiantly conjured up a meal for us. Two beers later, Roger was smiling again and the rigours of the day were already fading.

Nevertheless, there was no debate the following morning. A leisurely breakfast and a little skiing on and around the pistes was the order of the day. But the day after we continued our traverse northwards to the Lebanon's most famous ski resort, the Cedars, accompanied by Aram's mum and dad on skinny skis. It was another long day on undulating terrain, confirming the impression that Nordic equipment would defin-itely have been more appropriate than alpine. Only right at the end, as the sun was sinking, did we actually ski downhill, finishing with a brief but memorable descent in the dark, through the famous grove of immensely old cedar trees. During the afternoon, the sky had become veiled with cirrus and the wind rose steadily until it was blowing a full gale when we finally dropped off the plateau. The next morning it was snowing hard. Our itinerary had included an ascent of Mount Qurnat as Sawdā', the highest peak in Lebanon, but in thick fog the best we could do was skin up beside an inoperative drag-lift and ski down in curious new snow that felt more like sand than powder. It was, however, more than the disconsolate Rossignol demonstration team achieved. We had one more ski through the massive old trees, very beautiful in the new snow, and then called it a day. It was time to go sightseeing.

Camp on the Durung Drung glacier, Zanskar after the crevasse incident.

19

Zanskar: A Glance down Memory Lane

In the year of which I write I had only recently qualified as a guide, having worked as an aspirant for Dougal Haston in Leysin the previous summer. I was in full-time employment for almost the first time after several years of freedom as a self-indulgent itinerant climber and had been relieved to discover that the generous holidays of an LEA centre meant that I could still go to the Himalaya for a month in the summer. I had also not long been a father and I have to admit that coming home subsequently to find my son and heir did not recognise me gave me considerable food for thought.

Be that as it may, I arranged to meet Geoff Cohen and Des Rubens in Srinagar towards the end of July. It was only on arrival in that city that I realised we had not agreed a time or place for a rendezvous. It was purely by chance that, walking over a bridge in the middle of town I saw

95

a dead cow, legs in the air, floating downstream. I paused to watch it long enough to catch the sound of a distinctly Scottish accent issuing from a nearby houseboat. Moments later, with some relief, I was reunited with the rest of the Scottish Zanskar Expedition. Two more even-tempered and good-natured companions one could not hope to find. Whether they would say the same about me is another matter, but I do not recall a single cross word or argument the entire trip. Geoff and I had been climbing together in Scotland, the Alps, and the Himalaya for the previous ten years. Des, I had met in Gilgit two years before, though we had not yet climbed together. The pair of them had just spent a damp couple of weeks successfully climbing a peak of 5,800 metres, despite the monsoon, in the beautiful Wadwan valley in Kashmir.

Our choice of Zanskar for the second phase of their trip was based, in large part, on the belief that its climate would be unaffected by the monsoon. In this we were to be disappointed, for while Zanskar as a whole might receive only three inches of rain a year, the mountains straddling the watershed with Kishtwar attract a great deal of orographic cloud and significant snowfall in the summer months. The other reason for our choice of venue, however, was simply the desire to explore rather than climb a specific peak. This meant we could do without the expense of an official permit and a liaison officer; and while many expeditions had been to the west side of the Kishtwar Himal, the east side was terra incognita from a climbing point of view.

Like most Himalayan journeys this one started in a bus, a vehicle built for half the number of passengers it actually carried and with seats designed for passengers several inches shorter than us. It took us from the forests and meadows of Kashmir over the Zoji La into a dry, arid Tibetan landscape, reaching the little town of Kargil as the sun set. A fortuitous meeting with the local bank manager led to a comfortable night in sleeping bags on the roof of his house. The morning found us clambering into the back of an open-topped truck which we thought we were sharing with sacks of rice, a goat and some chickens, until the engine started and we were joined by twenty other passengers. Three hours and some fifty kilometres later we reached the village of Panikar, the end of the driveable road. Here, in due course, we were joined by Hassan, an impassive ponyman with two horses, each accompanied by a foal, who had agreed to carry our bags for the four-day journey to the top of the Pensi La. As so often, the distance travelled each day seemed remarkably short to sahibs impatient to reach the mountains. But the foals needed to suckle their mothers at regular intervals and Hassan liked to spend his afternoons helping other ponymen shoe their animals. This process was a far cry from the quiet skill of a farrier in Europe. Instead, it was a social event relying heavily on the presence of excitable onlookers to lasso, wrestle to the ground and sit on each struggling beast, while nails were driven into its hooves. It was a sport much enjoyed by everyone but the horse.

There was much else to wonder at and enjoy on the walk in. The dry, unpolluted air made for an extraordinary purity and clarity in the light, especially at each end of the day when the sun was low. There were fabled blue poppies, somehow surviving the fierce heat in the shade of undercut boulders. There were views of Nun and Kun, the twin 7,000-metre peaks of this region, and glimpses of rock walls reminiscent of Piz Badile. Above all, there were people, mostly Buddhist, in undyed homespun woollen garments even in the height of summer, the women wearing colourful coral and turquoise jewellery and elaborate leather head-dresses. There was the polite curiosity of the child monks who visited us one afternoon from Ringdom Gompa, their hilltop monastery, and the touching assumption of other children, playing with our ice axes, that they must be a form of plough. It felt a magical place, little touched by the twentieth century, quite unlike anywhere we had been before.

On the summit of the Pensi La, in a valedictory gesture, Hassan insisted on lighting a cowdung fire to brew up a last cup of tea before he headed home. To reciprocate we cracked open our hill-food to offer him a Ritz biscuit. For the previous three days, emulating Shipton and Tilman, we had been living on tsampa. This is a flour made from roasted barley which needs only the addition of hot water to be edible, rather like cous cous. With little in the way of vegetables or spices to enliven it, the tsampa had been heavy going and we were not sorry to move on to our mountain rations. Another urgent incentive to start eating was the weight of our packs. As we made a descending traverse from the pass on to the dry ice of the Durung Drung glacier, we were bowed under loads of at least thirty-five kilos. We had done everything to reduce weight. The three of us were sharing a lightweight two-man tent, we had just the one 9-millimetre rope between us, hardware was restricted to a few nuts and three or four pegs and we did not have harnesses, improvising with tape slings for glacier travel and abseils. But we had food and fuel for three weeks and there is a limit to how little food you can survive on in the mountains. We were verging on the skeletal as it was when, much later, we finally reached the chai-shops of Padam.

As we bade farewell to Hassan and his little posse, I was suddenly aware that no one else in the whole world knew exactly where we were or where we were going; and Hassan, shaking his head mournfully, clearly believed we would never be seen again. We were not very sure where we were going, ourselves. It was only a week or two before leaving the UK that I had been sent a Japanese sketch map that included the east side of the Kishtwar Himal, and it was only in Srinagar that we had decided to make for the Pensi La and the Durung Drung glacier. There was a powerful sense of venturing into the unknown. Zanskar itself had only been opened to westerners two years before, for the first time since Partition, and we knew of no climbing at all in the region south of Nun Kun. It required a level of commitment which we took for granted then but which is all but unknown today, when the expectation of clients or loved ones is that we will carry a satellite phone or radio or, at the very least, an emergency beacon when venturing into the wild. I remember being excited rather than disturbed by the prospect of being so totally out on a limb. Should anything go wrong we would be very much on our own.

In the event, it did not take long for something to go wrong. A few hours' walk up the Durung Drung, where the dry glacier became snow covered, we cached some of our food by a prominent boulder to lighten our loads. Soon afterwards, we entered a crevasse zone and roped up. After skirting a number of holes and cautiously crossing others I found myself confronted by an area where the edge of the crevasse was not obvious, despite probing, or even the direction in which it was running. 'Watch me here', I called out to Des turning round and giving him, I thought, a moment in which to tighten up the rope. Then I took a step forward and found myself falling through space. Instead of the rope coming taut, I fell about twenty feet and landed on my back with a splash in a pool of water. I did not appreciate the soaking at the time but the water almost certainly saved me from injury. I shouted but there was no reply, the sound of my voice swallowed up by glistening, dimpled walls of vertical ice. The only light came from the ragged hole I had made in the snow bridge above.

It was dark, cold and wet and I was beginning to shiver. No one came to the edge and, suddenly, I felt very much alone. With numb fingers, I attached prusik loops to the rope and set about climbing up it. Luckily I had spent the previous summer teaching clients this very skill. Ten minutes later I emerged, panting, to find Geoff and Des simply sitting on their rucksacks. Exhausted by heat and altitude they seemed totally uninterested in my plight. Remonstration about the slack in the rope elicited no response. Grumpily, and rather nervously now, I moved on to reach a place safe enough to camp, though still surrounded by crevasses. My priority was to dry my clothes while the sun was still high in the sky. To this day, I do not know quite why I was allowed to fall so far. Recently, climbing with Geoff in the Alps, I asked him about it, to discover that he has no recollection of the event whatsoever. On the other hand, I am reassured that my own vivid memory is not pure fabrication – and memory is known to play strange tricks sometimes – by a photo showing me standing outside the tent clad only in T-shirt, underpants and a pair of bright red over-boots, the sum total of my spare clothing. It was only when I put on those over-boots that I discovered, carefully written around the inside, the words, 'Made with love in the Tyn y Waen Himalayan Equip-ment Works'. That made my heart lurch; though on this occasion I was probably missing Netti more than she was missing me. She spent one of the best summers on record driving around the Highlands from farm to farm, baby on the back seat, working as a locum for the vet in Fort William.

At all events, the next day Geoff languished in the tent nursing a sore head while Des and I attempted the steep ice face of a small peak over-looking our camp. Today, a click of the mouse brings up numerous images of the Durung Drung glacier taken by cyclists and motor bikers crossing the Pensi La. On some of them this peak is visible on the true left bank, though much of the face is now rock.

A promising start, scrunching over crisp well-frozen snow, was brought to an abrupt halt by a huge uncrossable bergschrund, invisible from below, running the width of the face. Tails between our legs, we were back at camp by midday. We fared better the following morning. Geoff was recovered and we made straight for the obvious col at the foot of the west ridge. This required axes, crampons and the rope for some awkward rock steps and a couple of abseils. On one side of the ridge the orange granitic rock was warm to the touch, on the other the cracks were full of ice, and Dachstein mitts were swiftly pulled back on. By noon we were on top enjoying spectacular views westward to the magnificent Sickle Moon 6,570 metres, the dominant peak of the Kishtwar Himal, and north towards Nun Kun, savouring that special frisson that comes with knowing that, almost certainly, no one had ever been there before. With remarkable lack of imagination, we called it Viewpoint Peak but it did reveal a feasible approach to another higher peak on the same watershed ridge. The sketch map showed it to be 6,560 metres and although it did not look as high as that, relative to Sickle Moon, it was an attractive objective.

Reaching it the next day was not straightforward. From the col of Viewpoint we downclimbed, with tent, food and fuel for five days, 200 metres of steep snow, pitching with ice-screw belays when it turned to ice, to reach a snow basin at the head of the Prul glacier. Crossing this basin, just above a huge icefall, we set off up a rock spur which gave nearly three-hundred metres of exhilarating rock climbing with plentiful holds on steep but solid granite. The setting was as wild and remote as one could wish for, the gaping crevasses and fang-like pinnacles of the icefall snapping at our heels. At its top, the spur petered out into a snow slope too soggy and full of water under the afternoon sun to risk venturing on. Instead, we used our axes as mattocks to level an unpromising bank of shale into a platform. While pitching the tent, the bottom section of one of the poles dropped off and went tinkling forever down a nasty couloir flanking the spur. For the remainder of the trip that corner of the tent had to be propped up on a rock or a rucksack. The next four days were frustrating. The weather was never really bad, but it snowed lightly on and off much of the time and the cloud would lift briefly, only to fall again when we tried to move up. After two days we decided to move camp to a safer and more comfortable site at the bottom of the spur. Geoff's report mentions an abseil down the wrong side of the spur, which consumed a few hours. Since I have no memory of the incident, it seems fair to assume that I was responsible for this route-finding faux pas. On the fourth day, leaving Des in the tent feeling poorly, Geoff and I crossed back over to the Durung Drung, labouring in several inches of new snow, to fetch more food from the cache.

Finally, we awoke to a morning with pockets of blue sky and rapidly clearing mist below us. Leaving the tent behind but carrying bivvy gear, we set off for the summit. Back up the rock spur, not so pleasant plastered with snow, up the slopes above and into more mixed terrain of rock and ice, we gained height steadily to reach an upper cwm where we had originally hoped to camp. Above, a broad couloir of steep but firm, kickable *névé* brought us to the summit ridge. Almost simultaneously, the mist rolled in, the wind rose and temperatures plummeted. In a matter of minutes ice was forming on eyebrows and beards and we had passed hurriedly from T-shirts to wearing everything we possessed. There was nowhere flat enough to call a bivvy site so we pressed on along a knife edge of a ridge, snow and rock alternating, towards the feature we had called from afar the Grande Gendarme. This called for some pitched climbing and on the far side of it, on a vague levelling, we stopped for the night. It was not a comfortable bivouac. Snow fell, light but persistent, most of the night, pressing the cold clammy nylon of the Zdarsky sack against our faces and making it difficult to breathe. We all woke from an uneasy doze with headaches. Packing up was a stiff, cautious affair as we crammed wet sleeping bags into our sacks and struggled to put on frozen boots, terrified of dropping one. As we did so, the clouds parted to reveal Sickle Moon and a snow-smothered array of other, nameless peaks. The clearing was brief but it was dramatic while it lasted, making us acutely aware of the drops beneath us, hundreds of metres on one side, a thousand on the other. Then the mist rolled in again. We roped up for a final steep step and in no time, it seemed, we were on top. It was something of an anticlimax. There was nothing to be seen and nothing to be done except begin the descent.

My memory of the next couple of days is even hazier than usual, for a very good reason. Geoff and Des were wearing helmets, heavy, bulky, fibreglass things. In my determination to save weight, I had opted to leave mine at home. Predictably, as we pulled the rope down after the first abseil, it was on to my head that a boulder the size of a football landed, fair and square. I fell to my knees, feeling extremely groggy and almost certainly concussed. I could still put one foot in front of the other but I was in no state to think for myself or make decisions. The others shepherded me carefully down, pitching most of the way. We bivouacked a second time just below the ridge and it took the whole of the next day to get back to the tent. I remember next to nothing of that descent apart from feelings of embarrassment at my stupidity and relief that I was in such capable hands. We were all glad, I think, to spend a day brewing up and recuperating while my head cleared. However, when it was still cloudy and snowing intermittently the morning after, we decided to call it a day.

We still had some food left but the idea of further exploration was no longer appealing. Travelling through the land of Zanskar and on to Lahul and Kulu seemed much more attractive (and, in the event, did not disappoint).

We called that second summit Delusion Peak, based on the fact that it was clearly nowhere near the height shown on the map, probably more like 6,000 metres than 6,560. However, we did not actually feel deluded in the slightest. Since our first sight of it from Viewpoint we had had only tantalising glimpses of the mountain, but it had been a demanding climb – serious rather than technically difficult, like one of the classic Zermatt ridges – and a peak to be proud of. We felt both pleased with ourselves for persisting, and privileged to have been allowed to climb it and return in one piece. We were ready to go.

The North Face of Annapurna II seen from the lower slopes of Annapurna IV.

20

Nepal: Annapurna II
with Dick Isherwood

In 1978 Dick Isherwood was living in Kathmandu, working for Save the Children. On a trek in the Manaslu region he had spotted a possible line on the North Face of Annapurna II which fired his imagination. It was not long since Messner and Habeler had climbed Hidden Peak (Gasherbrum I) in impeccable alpine style, so two-man expeditions were very much in vogue and, as it turned out, we met Doug Scott and Joe Tasker in Kathmandu trying to do the same on Nuptse. The fact that Annapurna II is just under 8,000 metres did not concern us in the slightest but it did make it highly unlikely anyone else would be on it. When Dick asked me to join him I jumped at the chance before stopping to consider how I was going to pay for it. As I was earning a pittance at the time as an outdoor pursuits instructor and had a family to support, I pinned my hopes on winning a Churchill Fellowship in the adventure category. Thanks to references from Noel Odell and Peter Boardman I was shortlisted, but the makeup of the interviewing panel was distinctly old school and they were not at all impressed by the concept of two men alone on a big peak. I think Rum Doodle was their preferred style. I was sent away with a flea in my ear, regretting the cost of the train fare to London. At this point Dick offered to pay for the whole trip if I could get myself to Kathmandu, an act of generosity I reluctantly but gratefully accepted.

Dick was always highly organised in a quietly efficient way. Nothing important was ever forgotten or left behind. Years later, on a kayaking trip, I discovered he had detailed checklists for everything but rarely referred to them in public. In Kathmandu the shopping had been done and the formalities largely completed by the time I arrived. All I had to do was attend a final briefing in a ministry, the main purpose of which was to stress the importance of displaying the Nepali flag alongside the Union Jack on the summit. Neither of us were into flags, nor were we beholden to any sponsors, so we just nodded obligingly.

The walk in up the Marsyandi valley was a delight with such an informed companion. Dick had learnt Nepali which enabled him to haggle with villagers and banter with the porters as well as being a mine of information on flora and fauna. We persuaded our liaison officer that Base Camp should be in the village of Pisang where he could comfortably stay for the duration. Reaching Advanced Base Camp, where we would stay, proved more problematic. We knew from the report of a German expedition that there was an ideal plateau at about 5,000 metres, but we were not much over 4,000 metres when we came across a solitary, small cairn which the porters declared was our destination. Fortunately, the cloud came down at this point reducing visibility to a few metres. This allowed Dick to disappear up an ever-steepening hillside building cairns as he went, while I stayed with the porters who clearly believed we were following way-markers left by the Germans.

We had been at this camp only a couple of days, acclimatising, when our plans changed radically. The sight of a huge avalanche sweeping down the North Face obliterating the line of our proposed route caused a rapid rethink. The only viable alternative was to reach Annapurna II by traversing over Annapurna IV, which looked straightforward enough though it would not be a first ascent. However, that suddenly seemed less important than staying alive.

When we finally set out we reached 7,000 metres on the west ridge of Annapurne IV before being pinned down by bad weather for three days. It was a struggle to get that far. I was suffering from a mysterious malady, presumably a virus of some sort, which had no obvious symptoms apart from a total lack of energy. Although I could put one foot in front of the other, to my chagrin Dick had to do all the trail breaking, a task even he found exhausting. When the weather improved, giving us dramatic views of Machapuchare, it was clearly no more than a lull, and with food and fuel running low we beat a retreat. Predictably enough, the steep snow slopes we had toiled up were now smothered in soft, wind-blown new snow, creating an unavoidable avalanche trap. Almost immediately I released an avalanche several inches thick. I found myself self-arresting on a section of firm slab, which stopped moving even as the rest of the slope accelerated silently downwards. The next two or three hundred metres were safe, the snow scoured crampon-hard by the avalanche. Then we arrived at some little ice bulges running across the face, probably the line of a bergschrund, beneath which the debris had accumulated. Being of a suspicious nature when it comes to snow, I insisted on roping up. Dick passed the rope around his ice axe by way of belay but I made him adjust it so that his leg was braced against the shaft of the axe and the rope ran over his boot as well as round the axe, a New Zealand foot belay. I took one step downwards and the entire slope to a depth of nearly a metre broke away taking me with it. My full weight came abruptly on to the rope and Dick held me, but only just. We looked at each other, shaken, but said nothing – there seemed nothing to say – and continued on down without further incident, the avalanche having cleared the whole slope right to the bottom.

As I wearily removed crampons, neoprene overboots, and massively heavy leather double-boots, it was in the certain knowledge that I would not be rushing to put them on again. We could have sat at camp for another three weeks, or joined the liaison officer in the valley until an unseasonably late monsoon eventually ended, when we could have tried again with every chance of success. Other, braver climbers would have done so. But I was the father of two small children and my interest in the mountain had evaporated. Dick was equally unenthusiastic about the prospect of hanging around for another attempt and we headed for the fleshpots more relieved than disappointed.

The author on Ben Nevis in the 1960s.

21

Cambridge in the Sixties

2006 was the centenary of the Cambridge University Mountaineering Club. The committee of the club organised a dinner and solicited past members for contributions to a commemorative book. This piece was one of those contributions, although the book itself never materialised.

Whether the CUMC in the late sixties was more or less active than at other times I do not know. There was no one as well known as Nick Estcourt, who was just before my time, or Alan Rouse, who was just after. On the other hand, Ken Wilson's anthology *The Games Climbers Play* contains no less than four articles culled from the *Cambridge Mountaineering* journal of that era. Lectures in the Darwin site on Sidgwick Avenue could attract audiences of up to a hundred and we had the chance to listen to the wise, or more often irreverent, words of speakers like Eric Shipton, Tom Patey and a clean-cut young P.E. teacher called Doug Scott. The Freshers' Meet in Derbyshire easily filled a coach, but the six o'clock start on a Sunday morning and a three-hour drive each way ensured that a minibus was normally sufficient for outings to gritstone. The active membership in climbing terms was about twenty, though when I organised a weekend in Wales specifically to walk the Fourteen Threes, a totally different set of people emerged. For the demographically minded, the majority of the club's keenest members were on the science side rather than the arts, most came from the north, and women were conspicuous by their absence.

Twenty-five years later, Olly Overstall organised a reunion in North Wales. It was surprisingly well attended. For some, it transpired, climbing at Cambridge had been a hugely enjoyable but brief interlude before embarking on a career. But for many, mountaineering in one form or another continues to fill their leisure time and for Bob Barton and me, Cambridge proved to be an apprenticeship leading to the *Métier du Guide*. For all of us, however, it was an inherently dangerous period in which we learned many lessons the hard way and accidents did occur. The atmosphere was sombre at the first Tuesday teatime gathering one Lent term. Roger Wilson had been killed during the holiday period, when his gear ripped on the first pitch of *Haste Not* on White Ghyll. I remember all too clearly reading in a Swiss newspaper of the *chute mortelle* of Rollo Davidson and Michael Latham on the Biancograt. There but for the grace of God ... We were ambitious, competitive and, climbing 'not wisely but too well'; we had more than our fair share of near misses.

Of my immediate contemporaries, the leading personality was undoubtedly Mick Guilliard, a good-natured extrovert from Leek, hard by the Roaches, with an infectious laugh and an astonishing appetite for beer. We were in the same college and shared digs for a year so I knew him well and put him to bed more than once. I was never in the same league as a climber but I remember leading through, with trepidation, on an early ascent of *A Dream of White Horses* when fierce wind was blowing spume from the waves and the ropes billowed out in an arc on the final pitch. And again, on *White Slab* on a grey day with no-one else around and wreaths of mist drifting in and out behind the Far East Buttress, adding to the menace of the Black Cliff. And then there was our disastrous first alpine season, along with John Hamilton and Pete Hughes, when two of our three routes involved a forced bivouac and I nearly died when an abseil anchor failed.

Although the most accomplished and enthusiastic of us all, once he had qualified as a vet, Mick took up skiing and fell running and hung his rock shoes up for good.

John Cardy, with his shock of red hair and the enormous forehead of a boffin, was another distinctive figure. Neither of us was particularly strong in the arms and when we climbed together we usually chose our routes accordingly. We were in our element on the never-ending girdle of the West Buttress on Cloggy and tiptoed up *Bloody Slab* in good style; but when it came to *Cemetery Gates*, my hands were actually on the belay ledge when my fingers opened and I fell off. I was not to own a harness for another ten years, but I came to no harm and still have the garage nut that held me. Adrenaline propelled me back up on to the stance but I was less than pleased when Cardy announced on arrival that he was too pumped to lead the top pitch. With John, too, I spent several dank, autumnal days dangling nervously beneath ludicrous overhangs on limestone aid routes like *Castellan, Twilight, Hubris* and *The Prow*, all long since freed. John was something of an aficionado. I did not care for aid one bit but felt it was a necessary part of my education.

Rob Ferguson was a geographer whose keen interest in mountains was not just recreational. Unusual in his dislike of technical rock, Rob was a very confident snow and ice climber and became my mentor on early visits to Scotland and the Alps. When a large party was marooned on Tower Ridge at dusk, it was Rob who was dispatched into the infamous gap while the rest of us sang mournful dirges and yelled obscenities into the night to keep the cold at bay. It was Rob who led me up my first ice climb, *Three Gully Buttress*, cutting steps expertly with a straight-picked axe (though it was Bob Jones and Gordon McNair who saved my life, calmly fielding me when I tripped over my crampons on the descent to the *Carn Mor Dearg Arête*). And it was Rob who had the audacity to suggest attempting first the Fletschorn and then the Grosshorn north faces at a time when, the Triolet excepted, Brits just did not climb alpine ice and curved picks were yet to appear. Rob was always very organised. He was the only one of us properly shod when we bivvied on the crest of the Cuillin ridge one March prior to a traverse of the main ridge. I was wearing Hush Puppies because of an Achilles tendon problem. Denis Mollison was wearing baseball boots because they were all he had, and during the night it snowed …

Geoff Cohen was another more experienced mountaineer who initially took me under his wing. Geoff was, and is, a delightful person, famous for his inability to make decisions except, fortunately, when climbing. During my first long vacation we visited the northern highlands, cheekily knocking on Dr Tom Patey's door in Ullapool and spending a few nights in the bothy at the bottom of his garden. The doctor took us in person to the obscure Alladale Slabs and pointed us at the second ascent of the *Fiddler* on Ben Mor Coigach. One night we joined him in the pub at Inveroykel where closing time was unheard of. Patey was singing and playing his squeeze box into the wee small hours and beyond and while we crashed out in a barn nearby he was driving back across Scotland for morning surgery. The following winter Geoff and I teamed up again on Ben Nevis. The week in the Charles Inglis Clark hut had started badly when Gordon McNair, the President, was avalanched by a collapsing cornice while soloing an easy gully. As we struggled to splint his leg and put him on a stretcher brought up from the hut, we were all hit by another avalanche and swept further down Coire na Ciste in a tangled mess of bodies and equipment. In retrospect, we were extraordinarily ignorant to have been launching ourselves up snow gullies in semi-tropical conditions. By the end of the week, it was at least colder, but otherwise the weather was atrocious and everyone else was heading downwards as we set off for the North East Buttress. Then as now, this was regarded as a long, serious climb rather than a hard one, but it felt quite hard enough for me, chipping steps in earnest for the first time. The sense of commitment at the foot of the *Mantrap* in thick mist and a howling gale, the exhilaration of fighting our way over the summit, and the state of contented exhaustion in which we squelched our way down the boggy path in the dark to Fort William, were all new but were to become quite addictive for a few years. It may have been the same occasion that the police moved us on from a comfortable bivouac in a bus shelter. The night being dreadful and the cells full, they found a railway carriage for us instead, first class at that, with the stipulation that we vanish by seven in the morning.

While my friends were pushing their grades in Wales and the Lakes, the whole of my second long vacation was taken up by an expedition to the Hindu Kush. I was recruited by a group of ex-CUMC members – Alan Cormack, Dick Metcalfe and John Peck. Peck was a colourful figure with shoulder-length blond hair and an enormous beard, who lived in a garret in Spittalfields, producing what he called 'semi-pornographic' etchings. The overland journey to Pakistan in an old army truck was a six-week epic in which personal relations broke down almost as frequently as the vehicle. The mountains, when we finally reached them, felt like a rest cure by comparison. Before we could climb anything, however, we first had to rendezvous with Henry Day, whom we had last seen in the officers' mess of the Royal Engineers in Osnabruck. We had arranged to meet at our proposed Base Camp beside a lake near Sor Laspur in Chitral, but plans changed when we learned that a party of Austrians were at the same site. Having no permit, it seemed tactful to go elsewhere and we ended up on the other side of the watershed in Swat. Unfortunately, there was no way of letting Henry know. In the event, Alan and I missed him by a day, after a week's journey over untrodden glaciers involving rock-fall, an almost fatal crevasse incident and some scary river crossings. I was learning all the time and discovering that mountain travel could be just as rewarding, and as hazardous, as actual climbing. However, my most vivid memory is of meeting, near the lake, a dignified but courteous Chitrali horseman, a falcon on his wrist, a spaniel running to heel and a retainer walking behind carrying a musket and a bag of provisions. Subsequently we climbed a number of peaks just under 6,000 metres and I acquired a taste for that sort of exploratory mountaineering which has never left me.

When Dick Isherwood asked me to join a small team going to Chitral the next year, I jumped at the chance. At the time, Dick was one of the best rock climbers in the country as well as a formidable powerhouse in big mountains. In his company, an awe-struck youth, I found myself rubbing shoulders in Wales and the Peak with god-like figures such as Crew, Boysen and the wonderfully voluble Holliwell brothers. On that trip I learned a great deal about alpinism from Dick, and from Colin Taylor too, but above all I learned that in the mountains you must seize your chances with both hands. We oh-so-nearly climbed Thui II, a beautiful peak at the head of the Yarkhun valley, but we bivouacked early and the weather broke during the night. We were prevented from making a second attempt by our liaison officer, an extremely unpleasant man who later had us turned back at the Khyber Pass because of 'currency irregularities' and, I learned later, did his best to have me thrown in jail.

Skiing was not a sport that appealed to climbers in those days, but I had been on a couple of school ski trips and I was inspired by a picture in

Alan Blackshaw's *Mountaineering* of a mountain tent guyed down with skis in a blizzard. Chris Barry was equipped with my mum's edgeless wooden skis from the thirties, given a day's tuition in Coire Cas and then dragged off over the Cairngorm plateau to Ben Macdui. I was hooked even if Chris was not, and the next winter a Land Rover-full of us, including Tim Nulty, an American economist who had been enormously helpful in Pakistan the previous summer, the bohemian Peck and David Gundry, companion on many an escapade before and after, set off on a three day marathon drive to the Bernese Oberland. Christof Lehrner, a guide in the Lötschental, lent us a straw-filled barn to stay in, warmed from below by cattle and sheep, and a day tour in his company taught us a lot about skins and kick-turns, though not, alas, how to ski difficult snow. Even snapping my brand-new skis, four days stormbound in the unguarded Hollandia hut and a sightless descent in total whiteout did not diminish my enthusiasm for ski mountaineering.

Times change but topography does not and Cambridge has never been the ideal location for a climber. Purpose-built climbing walls were still in the future, but the notion of training for performance must have been gaining ground, for no sooner had the old lime kiln at Cherry Hinton, with its carefully chipped if rather slippery holds, been blown up on safety grounds, than the energetic development of disused railway bridges began. The arrival of Harold Gillespie and Mick Geddes from Edinburgh with tales of the Currie Wa's must have had something to do with it.

Of course, generations of Cambridge climbers had found adventure aplenty on their doorstep, at night. Geoffrey Winthrop Young with his pre-First World War *Roof Climbers Guide to Trinity* was only perpetuating a tradition, which found its finest expression in the thirties with Whipplesnaith's *The Night Climbers of Cambridge*. The sixties' contribution to the genre by Hederatus did not match the whimsy and humour of that classic, but it reflects the secretive nature of the activity that I never knew who wrote it. For myself, I loved the heightened awareness created by the dark and the illicit, the sense of being privy to a totally different night-time world when the only other signs of life in the silent town were perhaps a solitary light high up in a tower window or the hooting of an owl. Most of the keenest climbers of my time, though, did not much care for night climbing, with its need for stealth and silence. The metallic clink of a karabiner or the briefest flash of a headtorch could be enough to betray one to a prowling bulldog and the authorities suffered from a sense of humour failure when it came to night climbing, especially on *Kings'*.

Kings' is the most famous route in Cambridge and it certainly has some unique situations, but *John's* is the better climb. It offers laybacking, bridging, a delicate slab, and a final strenuous overhang in a superb position; there is even an easy descent if you have played your cards right. Dick Isherwood described it as, 'The finest Severe in England', and he was probably right. One ambition I never achieved was the Senate House Leap. Chris Barry had a room ideally situated high up in Caius. One night we used a plank to measure the distance and practised standing jumps in the corridor. Neither of us could ever quite make the chalk mark on the floor and discretion proved the better part of valour; though on another occasion, after a dinner, Chris used the same plank to walk across.

Night-climbing skills could be deployed in other contexts, too. During the Europe-wide student unrest of 1968 there was a sit-in at the Old Schools which I was able to drop in and out of as I chose. It was good fun, though I cannot for the life of me remember what we were protesting about. During my final year my wife-to-be, Netti, was at Newnham. Visitors had to be out of the college by ten o'clock which seemed unduly restrictive so we kept a rope under her bed. Abseiling out of the window into the garden was given an added frisson by a don occupying the room below.

I suppose I had a rather cavalier attitude towards my degree. Hours spent gazing out of the university library at clouds and trees, along with subversive texts by Thoreau, Richard Jeffries and Henry Williamson, convinced me that whatever I did in the future was going to be out of doors. In my fourth, final year the university careers department, mystified by this attitude, arranged only one interview for me, with a firm of rubber traders in Malaysia. Fortunately help was at hand in the form of Noel Odell. Odell was in his eighties then, but still very fit and spry. He had a weakness for crumpets and used to call round at teatime, usually on a Monday, to compare notes about the weekend. On one occasion, staying at the Pen y Gwryd hotel for a Climbers' Club dinner, he had walked over the Glyders on Saturday and up Snowdon on the Sunday and was full of it when we met. Mick Guilliard, who had also been up to Wales, had already told me at breakfast that the weather had been so vile that they had spent the entire weekend in Wendy's café and the Padarn ... It was Odell who introduced me to the Alpine Club, driving me up to

London in his Mini a number of times and later proposing me for membership. Like many of his generation, he was a great raconteur and I loved listening to his stories of Everest and Nanda Devi.

From Odell I learned that the British Antarctic Survey employed mountaineers for its fieldwork and that Sir Vivien Fuchs was giving a public lecture the following week. One thing led to another and a year 'on the ice' with a dog team made it even less likely that I could settle into an office job or endure the rigours of the chalk-face. Eventually, I drifted into instructing and guiding almost by default but I have never regretted it – the boundary between work and play often blurring. Looking back, I can see that my years at Cambridge were not just enormous fun, but they gave me a profession, a spouse and some lifelong friends. What more could one ask of a university education?

III

ISSUES

A fence built for no obvious purpose other than a generous subsidy.

22

Fencing in the Uplands

Living and working in Snowdonia, nothing has upset me more in recent years than the proliferation of fencing high up in the mountains. Just as the right to roam has become a reality in law, the space in which we can roam has been circumscribed as never before. In the eighties fences suddenly appeared above the *Devil's Kitchen* and on the summit ridges of Foel Goch and Mynydd Perfedd in the Glyderau, on Foel Fras in the Carneddau, and on Moel Cynghorion and Moel Eilio in the Snowdon group. Later, there was a new wave of fencing all over the Moelwynion from Siabod to Stwlan, on Snowdon from Pen y Pass over the Horns high up on to Crib Goch, and from near Clogwyn Station right down the north-west ridge toward Llanberis, to mention only the most obvious. And then the National Trust embarked on a major fencing project on their new estates of Hafod y Llan and Gelli Iago. Wherever you go in Snowdonia there is now fencing.

Why should all these fences suddenly be deemed necessary when previously they were not? It seems that while one farm has been reducing stocking densities in order to qualify for an agri-environmental subsidy, its neighbour has continued to over-graze to receive the maximum headage payment. It is a ridiculous situation but only a temporary one. The suggestion that this might be an opportunity to re-introduce traditional shepherding, someone actually walking the land with dogs on a regular basis to prevent the drift of sheep from one farm to the greener grass of the other, fell on deaf ears. Fences are so much simpler, especially when the grant system can be manipulated to make a tidy profit. (I am told on good authority that a fence can be erected by a contractor for three pounds per metre while grants are available at nine pounds a metre.) Most farmers cannot see what all the fuss is about. Fencing is a tried and tested way of managing stock so why not extend it further up the mountainside if the money is there to pay for it? Besides, they have every right to do what they like with their land.

I do not agree. Leaving aside the question of whether any man can 'own' a mountain, we, the public, pay taxes from whence cometh subsidies and we have a stake in how land is treated. Fences in the uplands strike at the heart of what mountains have to offer, undermining what Harold Drasdo once called, 'those two ancient, anarchic, subversive values – beauty and freedom'. A key phrase in the 1949 National Parks Act was that Britain's parks should exist to 'preserve and enhance the natural beauty of the landscape.' The historian, G.M. Trevelyan, one of the founders of the YHA and a prime mover in the campaign for national parks in this country in the nineteen-thirties, wrote this:

> 'Civilized man feels the desire and need for the wildness and
> greatness of untamed, aboriginal nature, which his predecessors
> did not feel … By the side of religion, by the side of science,
> by the side of Poetry and Art, stands Natural Beauty, not a rival
> to these, but as the common inspirer and nourisher of them all,
> and with a secret of her own beside.'

But what is natural beauty? Can it be defined when, notoriously, 'beauty is in the eye of the beholder', when social background, personal preoccupation or our mood of the moment all play a part in determining whether we even notice something, be it a vista or a leaf, let alone allow ourselves to be moved by it? Yet, in terms of landscape, most people would agree, I think, that beauty has something to do with harmony, with things fitting, being all of a piece.

Harmony can relate to colours, shapes, materials, sounds. Bright orange anoraks or tents disturb harmony in the hills temporarily, as can the deafening violence of low-flying jets or the more insistent pounding of helicopters. A fence disturbs it permanently (or for twenty to thirty years anyway). It is not so much that fences are man-made or even that wire is an unnatural material as that they run in dead-straight lines never found in nature and when they are barbed, as they usually are, or worse still, elec- trified like some in the Moelwynion, they convey a hostile, aggressive message, not just to sheep. (In fact, barbed wire is quite unnecessary to restrain sheep, and cattle are rarely grazed high up these days.) In short, a fence is an ugly and often unnecessary artefact imposed arbitrarily and insensitively on the landscape.

By contrast, a stone wall uses natural materials, makes use of natural features on the ground and looks organic and in keeping within the landscape. Having said that, modern wallers tend to pride themselves on the geometric straightness of their work whereas old walls were rarely straight; and it has to be recognised that the majority of existing walls date from the Enclosure Acts and are a reminder that what Marion Shoard has called 'the theft of the countryside' was a comparatively recent event. Nevertheless, a well-built, lichen-encrusted wall can be the object of admiration and a source of pleasure in a way that no fence will ever be.

Freedom is the other crucial value in our relationship with the great out- doors. Our everyday lives are constrained not only by the need to earn a living and maybe the desire to raise a family, but equally by routine and convention. Where we can go, what we can do, when we can do it, even what we can wear are all dictated to us much of the time. We have remark- ably little real choice in how we live from day to day. But, like *The Manchester Rambler*, we may be wage slaves from Monday to Saturday but we can be free men on Sunday, and the moors and the mountains beckon.

Gavin Maxwell put it beautifully in his foreword to *Ring of Bright Water* when he described Camusfearna and places like it as symbols, 'Symbols for me and for many of freedom, whether it be from the prison of over-dense communities and the close confines of human relationships, from the less complex incarceration of office walls and hours, or simply freedom from the prison of adult life and an escape into the forgotten world of childhood, of the individual or the race.'

Even more important, however, is a need for physical space, for exercise, for clean air and for direct contact with nature. Only in the last two-hundred years have most people in the west come to lead lives so cut off from the natural world and the elements of earth, air, sun and water. Many of the world's problems can be traced back to the loss of any sense that we are, as individuals, a part of nature, a part of a global ecosystem. There is a widespread need for places where there are few other people and few physical restrictions and where we can re-connect with nature, Mother Earth, Gaia, call her what you will. Gavin Maxwell asserts, 'I am convinced that man has suffered in his separation from the soil and from the other living creatures of the world; the evolution of his intellect has outrun his needs as an animal, and as yet he must still, for security, look long at some portion of the earth as it was before he tampered with it.'

Yet in Snowdonia fences are everywhere now, along with quad bikes for transporting the materials. They are a physical denial of freedom to roam and a disruption of harmony in the landscape. Open places scarcely exist as we follow well-trodden paths from stile to stile along a fence-line. Beauty and freedom, both of them diminished and diminishing ... how could this have come about in a national park created with such vision and idealism sixty years ago?

I will not catalogue again the absurdities of the Common Agricultural Policy or the destructive short-sightedness of government subsidies. That has been documented in heart-breaking detail by Graham Harvey in *The Killing of the Countryside*. But I do lament the values espoused by self-styled guardians of the countryside. It has become the fashion recently amongst spokesmen for hill farmers to speak of the land as a factory. 'How would you like it', they ask, 'if I were to walk unbidden across your factory floor?' That phrase speaks volumes about mechanistic farming practice and an all-too prevalent attitude towards the living earth and animals reared on it. Were farmers to regain the use of their legs and actually walk their land as they did until recently, it would be to the benefit of the land, their animals and their own health.

Yet for a lot of people, not just visitors from the towns, but local residents too and even, I readily admit, some farmers, mountains and wild places remain in some indefinable way, special. Perhaps it is because they remind us that there is more to life than the relentless pressure to consume. If we but slow down sufficiently and open our eyes we may realise what Jim Perrin calls, 'moments of shimmering clarity of perception' when, briefly, we transcend our everyday selves. Perhaps, if we were less shy about our feelings, more prepared to stand up and be counted, we might even call these places sacred. We would not be alone. Kailas in Tibet, Machapuchare in Nepal, Shivling in India are venerated by huge numbers. In Japan there are over three hundred sacred mountains. In Bhutan none of the 7,000-metre peaks are open to climbers because the King puts the wishes and spiritual welfare of local villagers before dollars. Our forbears, long ago, must have felt the same. All over Snowdonia burial cairns dating back four thousand years are to be found on the summits, reflecting the reverence once felt for these high places. And still felt, if not often openly expressed, by many today.

For hundreds if not thousands of years the hills of Wales were grazed by sheep, goats and cattle, controlled by shepherds and their dogs. Fencing with wire was a creation of the twentieth century and only in the last twenty years has it been extended above the mountain wall on to the high tops. We do not have to accept that it is here to stay. Posts and wire can be taken down and removed as soon as the anomalies of the subsidy system have been resolved. Once down, a moratorium could be imposed on both fencing and the use of machines on all land over 600 metres. Let us allow high land to be wild land once more and accord the mountains the respect they deserve.

Wind turbine near Bala.

23

What Price Windpower?

Britain is a densely populated island in which the vast majority of people lead urban lives largely divorced from the natural world and the realities of sun, rain, wind, moon, stars and the rhythm of the seasons. For this reason, the countryside and our few remaining areas of relatively wild moorland and mountain are precious to many. They provide opportunities, at weekends and holiday times, not just for fresh air and exercise, but for a reconnection with nature and spiritual renewal. It was recognition of this need that led, after a long campaign, to the establishment of ten national parks in England and Wales during the early 1950s.

Despite this, over the last sixty years the uplands of Britain have been disfigured by a succession of agricultural schemes and 'improvements'. Blanket planting of conifers, drainage of peat bogs, dredging of rivers, reseeding of hay meadows, grubbing up of hedges, four-wheel drive roads right to the summits, fences where none existed before – the list of destruction and modification of the land is endless. Although motivated by a desire to increase productivity at any cost, these changes were driven not by market forces but by government (usually Common Agricultural Policy) subsidies. Most of these schemes, and certainly the scale on which they were implemented, are now regarded as a disastrous mistake and a misuse of public funds.

The current enthusiasm for wind farms comes into exactly the same category, but it threatens to be more damaging to our wild landscapes than anything that has been inflicted on them so far. It is not an uncontested process. The decision to build thirty-nine turbines, each over a hundred metres high on Cefn Croes in Mid Wales was described by the Bishop of Hereford as an act of vandalism equal to the destruction of the Buddhist statues of Bamiyan by the Taliban. He is far from alone in his view, yet the Department of Trade and Industry has made the building of wind-farms hugely attractive to investors and developers. Not only are direct grants available for construction, but also the electricity produced can be sold at three times the normal market price. As power companies have to buy a fixed proportion of their electricity from renewable sources, they are obliged to pay the inflated price for it. Small wonder developers are queuing up to apply for wind farm licenses.

However, what really puts the pressure on wilder, upland parts of Britain is the Department of Trade and Industry's (DTI) insistence on awarding contracts on an economically competitive basis without regard to landscape implications. In other words, a windy hilltop site on the edge of a national park will be preferred to a less windy but still perfectly viable 'brownfield' site. Hills are far from essential for wind generation. Denmark is almost entirely flat, yet gleans thirty per cent of its energy from wind power. One does not have to be opposed to wind energy per se, to object to it being produced in our wildest landscapes.

To add insult to injury, government planning policy guidelines on renewable energy (1993) actively encourage local planning authorities to override Town and Country Planning legislation designed to protect the countryside. What is more, all offshore wind projects and any large-scale on-land projects are subject to planning approval from the DTI rather than local authorities, effectively stifling opposition.

In its desire to be seen to be doing something about global warming, the government has adopted a carrot and stick approach to the electricity industry and it has been supported, unusually, by the campaigning organisations Greenpeace and Friends of the Earth. Not surprisingly, objections from the Council for National Parks, the Ramblers Association, the Council for the Protection of Rural Wales and innumerable local pressure groups have been swept aside. It has become politically incorrect to oppose wind energy.

As a result, the last remnants of wild land in Britain are being industrialised at a frightening rate. Industrialise is not too strong a word for what is happening. The term 'wind farm' is actually a euphemism for a power-station, which may not be polluting in terms of emissions, but is visible from twenty miles away, audible for a mile, requires half an acre of concrete footing for each turbine and means the building of access roads and power-lines in formerly remote locations. The effect on the actual fabric of the land cannot easily be undone, any more than the effect on the wider landscape of countless rotating blades. It is all depressingly reminiscent of the sixties and seventies, when huge swathes of wild land in Scotland and Wales were planted with conifers as tax-breaks for pension funds and millionaires. Their value as timber has been negligible, the detrimental effect on the landscape and what can live there, enormous. And even when abandoned they, like the windmills, will remain there for many, many years.

None of this is of concern to the owners of the Moel Maelogan wind farm in North Wales. Highly visible from many parts of the Snowdonia National Park, this small-scale local initiative on the part of three farmers received planning permission thanks to a wave of public sympathy following the foot and mouth crisis. Two years later, predictably, they wished to enlarge it from three turbines to fourteen. As an apparent concession to the planners, they have reduced the number of new turbines from eleven to nine, and their height from ninety metres to eighty. Curiously, this has persuaded the Countryside Council for Wales to withdraw its objection, arousing suspicion that political pressure was brought to bear. The revised scheme was approved and (consequently) opened the floodgates to further applications.

And to what end? At present, there are over a thousand wind turbines in the UK, a high proportion of them in Mid Wales where the landscape has already been devastated. Two hundred and fifty are visible from the summit of Pumlumon alone. Yet the DTI estimated that 10,000 would be needed merely to supply sixty per cent of its overall target for renewable energy by 2010. The mind boggles. The remarkably rapid development of offshore wind farms offers a ray of hope. Although not to everyone's liking, they are far less contentious visually and environmentally. Yet inland contracts have been awarded, planning applications are in the pipeline. The juggernaut is not easily halted.

Meanwhile, as a nation our electricity consumption keeps in step with inflation, rising steadily. As a result, the percentage of electricity being produced by renewables is actually falling. The government blithely predicts that the numbers of cars on the roads will continue to increase, that air travel will grow ever more popular, as if these are givens that cannot be altered. Global warming continues apace. The development of renewable energy from wind, sun, wave and tide is vitally important, but not as crucial as curbing our consumption and conserving energy. There is so much that could be done if the political will was there, but alas, it is not. Seen in this context, wind farms in the uplands are mere window-dressing; government applying an eye-catching technical fix, rather than tackling the real problem. In the meantime, our finest landscapes become more mutilated by the day.

Beauty in the landscape is a highly subjective issue, says Greenpeace. 'Being visible is not necessarily the same as being intrusive.' And a turbine can be seen as an object of beauty. In isolation, yes, perhaps. In hundreds, definitely not. For the farmers at Moel Moelogan as for the mandarins of the DTI, moorland and hills are simply unutilised empty spaces to be exploited. For others, they are places where space, silence, solitude can sometimes be experienced, where that elusive but important quality of wildness, or even wilderness, can be felt. For the poet R.S. Thomas moorland was like a church, a place to be accessed with the utmost respect. There are few places left in Britain that can still inspire that degree of reverence in the face of creation. If we are not careful there will soon be none.

Heli-skiers being dropped off high in the mountains.

24

A Day on the Haute Route

Not long ago I was guiding a group of friends from the Eagle Ski Club on the final stage of the famous Haute Route from Chamonix to Zermatt. Originally named the High Level Route by its nineteenth century British pioneers, the name was long ago purloined by the French and who would begrudge them this rare case of linguistic one-upmanship? At all events, we left the snug little Bouquetins refuge, unguarded but very well equipped, at first light. On skis, we skimmed across the hard frozen south-facing slopes overlooking the upper Arolla Glacier on a gradually descending traverse, like running a finger round a mixing bowl. We must have covered a kilometre in five minutes or less to reach flat ground in the middle of the basin where the sun, still low in the sky at the end of March, had failed to melt the surface and the snow was still soft and powdery. Skins on the base of our skis, heels released from the bindings, we made

127

our way towards the short but steep Col du Mont Brulé.

It was a cold, clear morning, still and quiet, the sun just catching golden rock at the top of the Sunrise Pillar on Mont Collon. We had the cirque to ourselves. Parties from the Vignettes hut would be making their way towards the Col de l'Evêque. Our Swiss friends from the night before had not yet emerged from the Bouquetins. We felt full of energy and expectation but also a kind of wonder at the perfection of it all.

Usually the Col du Mont Brulé is climbed with skis on packs and crampons on feet, but on this occasion no one had descended it either on foot or ski since the last snowfall two days before and a well-crafted skinning track zigzagged all the way to the top. After twenty kick-turns in quick succession even the less proficient were becoming confident. It was a perfect opportunity to practise and master a crucial ski-touring skill.

On the far side we were in Italy and confronted by a broad open slope of perfect powder. With varying degrees of style and elegance we linked our turns, striving for that rhythmic, almost sensuous fluency that is so addictive, then a long fast traverse down into the heart of the Tsa de Tsan glacier basin. Ahead, between the rock walls of the Tête Blanche and the broken, crevassed slopes of the Tête de Valpelline, lay the Col de Valpelline, gateway to the promised land of the Mischabel. Somewhere below, to the south, was the Aosta hut; to the north was the Col des Bouquetins, now a steep corniced snow slope, though twenty years ago there was a small but mobile sérac band best given a wide berth.

Time for sun specs and a hat. Skins back on the skis and we were off on the final 450-metre uphill pull. We were fit, acclimatized and the sun had not yet turned this glacier into the enervating cauldron it would become later. With time on our side and powder snow to ski, we had already decided to continue upwards from the col for another 250 metres in order to enjoy the delectable north-facing slope of the Tête de Valpelline before embarking on the grande finale of the Haute Route, the long descent of the Zmutt glacier, past the Stockji, under the North Face of the Matterhorn and on to the pistes of Zermatt.

We had been skiing for nearly an hour when we heard the first helicopter. Although mountaineers have perforce become accustomed to these machines being an integral part of the alpine environment, stocking huts and providing a speedy and efficient rescue service, sometimes they can still seem an intrusion, breaking the spell that allows us to become briefly a part of the mountain world. On this occasion my heart sank as the throbbing grew louder and a blue and white dragonfly circled the summit of the Tête de Valpelline. On a day like this it could mean only one thing – heli-skiers.

In Switzerland heli-skiing is regulated in so far as skiers have to be accompanied by a guide and it is restricted to some forty-odd landing zones or *places d'atterrissage* as they are called on the map. The Tête de Valpelline is not one of them but that problem is easily overcome by landing on the Italian side of the summit.

It is a curious perversity that heli-skiing is a booming industry. Just as, over the last thirty years since recycling has become widely regarded as desirable, disposable nappies have changed from being luxury items to absolute necessities, so concerns about the burning of fossil fuels and the contribution of CO_2 to global warming have led to holidays in South America, Australia and New Zealand selling as never before, while heli-ski operations in Canada cannot meet demand and are expanding into wilderness areas like Mount Waddington. For guides in the Swiss Valais, heli-skiing has become a significant source of employment any fine day after a snowfall in winter. Any hint of political correctness, it seems, provokes an illogical backlash in which there is a certain machismo in rubbishing received opinion, or else just a cynical abdication of any personal responsibility. Certainly, many skiers and mountaineers who have plenty of opportunity to experience first hand what is happening to the world's glaciers, seem more inclined to fiddle while Rome burns than to modify their activities or lifestyle.

However, in Europe, another valid objection to heli-skiing that does not really apply in, say, Canada, is the effect it has on other people's enjoyment of the mountains. The abrupt arrival of a helicopter off-loading a gang of people with more money than either sense or sensibility, not only destroys the ambience of a place, breaking what Ansel Adams described as 'that vital thread of perfection', but it also deprives ski-tourers who may have been skinning uphill for hours, of the reward of skiing untracked powder.

As we neared the crest of the Col de Valpelline and the tiny black cone of the Matterhorn, peeping above the horizon, grew and grew until we could see the whole wildly improbable peak, we were also subjected to wave after wave of skiers whooping their way down a slope which an hour earlier had been totally unmarked. One of ski touring's fairest prizes had been rudely snatched from us.

As we neared the summit the smell of aviation fuel lingered in the air. We could see chattering flocks of brightly dressed skiers, not even a bumbag between them, being marshalled by Swiss guides dressed all in black and wearing helmets, who looked more like stormtroopers than mountaineers. When they had departed we occupied the fore-summit, cautiously visited the dramatically exposed little pinnacle that is the true summit and started to remove the skins from our skis. Then the helicopter was back with yet another load. I was in the middle of folding a skin and did not feel inclined to rush the job. The helicopter pilot wasn't inclined to mess around, either – after all this was business and fuel costs money. He came straight on in and I dropped hastily to the ground clutching skis, sticks and skins. I lost my sun hat in the downdraught but I suppose that was better than my head. I was not amused. This time the guide was Italian and fortunately he seemed anxious rather than aggressive. While I smouldered, Dick Allen, with his usual charm and diplomacy, stepped in to defuse what could have become an international incident.

This was not the first time that I have had a mountain day ruined or drastically diminished by a throng of unthinking skiers encouraged into the mountains by guides interested only in easy money and the glamorous posturing of their role. Guides really earn their money when the weather is bad, which usually means poor visibility and high winds, neither of which are liked by pilots. Heli-skiing is essentially a fair-weather activity and most of the time it is money for jam as far as guides are concerned. Over the years I have had similar experiences on Monte Rosa, the Lysjoch, Pigne d'Arolla, Petit Combin, Ebnefluh and Petersgrat. The day after this incident as we skinned from the Stockhorn towards the Cima di Jazzi, we were once again subjected to the thud-thud-thud of helicopters flying backwards and forwards across our line of travel shuttling skiers on to the upper slopes of the Dufourspitze. The Swiss guides' typical response to complaint is unsympathetic, along the lines of 'these are our mountains, we can do what we like with them' and 'more fool you for going to mountains where heli-skiing is permitted.'

I have been a qualified guide for over thirty years now and, sadly, I have come to realise that many guides – not all, I hasten to add, but a fair proportion – do not value mountains as mountains or for a relation to them that goes beyond technical mastery, challenge and achievement. The mountain is simply a place of work to be exploited for cash. The ability to experience beauty in a landscape, to feel respect for what lives and grows there, and humility in the face of natural forces, if it ever existed, becomes blunted by familiarity. Communicating such feelings or creating situations in which they can occur have no place in a guide's training (except, possibly, in Norway, where the tradition of *friluftsliv* and the writings of Arne Naess are still influential).

I remember years ago being shocked and dismayed to discover how many fine climbs, not just the notorious Hornli Ridge on the Matterhorn, but routes like the Ryan-Lochmatter on the Plan, the Dent du Géant and the Mittellegi Ridge on the Eiger, were draped with hawsers to make climbing rock unnecessary. Small wonder, the fixed rope ethos is so prevalent in the greater ranges. And who puts the ropes there? The local guides, to make them more accessible to more people, which means more clients. The sports climbing revolution and the proliferation of bolts in the high mountains were driven, to a large extent, by the same people with the same motives; likewise, the metal clutter of *via ferrata* to provide cheap thrills for tourists. And it is guides, of all nationalities, who actively promote heli-skiing in Europe and seek to extend it more and more to third world venues. There is even a 'Heli-Haute Route' on offer.

I have done enough heli-skiing myself as a guide in New Zealand and Canada, to know that the helicopter ride in itself can be spectacularly exciting and, undeniably, a huge number of turns can be made if you have a helicopter for the day, or a week. But the tendency is for skiers to become caught up in a sort of consumerist frenzy in which quantity becomes more important than quality. The skiing becomes a kinaesthetic blur, an orgy of physical sensation a bit like binge drinking, in which no individual pitch or run stands out and the chief satisfaction is in achieving or exceeding so many thousands of metres of descent. By contrast, for the ski tourer, who spends most of the time going uphill, every pitch downhill, every turn almost, is something to be relished and consciously savoured. And skinning uphill is not time wasted. It is an opportunity to slow down, to notice, pay attention to and derive pleasure from the detail in the landscape – the cough of a chamois, the creak of a ptarmigan, the flashing, delicately striated plates of hoar frost that have grown on the snow overnight, the fan-like rays of light and shade that burst from behind a ridge just before the sun appears, the bright luminous green of lichen on the fissured bark of Arolla pine in the valley below – all those small but important things that give texture and substance to a mountain day.

As for the view, it is a truism that rewards in all spheres of life are in direct proportion to the effort expended. The view from col or summit enjoyed by the ski-mountaineer will be qualitatively different to that of a person who has been jetted there with no effort whatsoever. 'There is a beauty that must be paid for in the currency of suffering', wrote Arnold Lunn long ago. A bit over the top, I admit, but any mountaineer will know what he meant. Your average heli-skier would think he was barking mad.

The trouble is, my pleasure does not impinge on that of heli-skiers; but their pleasure most certainly does affect mine. And I am by no means alone. Ski *randonnée* may be a minority activity compared to piste skiing, but it has become hugely popular in the Alps in recent years. A combination of this recreational lobby and the European environmental movement is creating a climate in which heli-skiing in Switzerland and Italy just could be banned, as it is in France and Austria. The sooner the better!

The staircase leading up to the Konkordia hut in the Bernese Oberland.

25

Cri de Coeur from the Alps

The Aletsch Glacier, which flows out of the Bernese Oberland into the Rhône valley in Western Switzerland, is the longest glacier in the Alps. It is fed by a number of ice-streams emanating from peaks like the Abeni Fluhe, Jungfrau, Mönch, Fiescherhorn and Grünhorn, most of them over 4,000 metres. The point at which these tributaries merge to form the Aletsch is a plain of snow two kilometres wide known as Konkordiaplatz. At the geographical heart of the Bernese Oberland and a UNESCO World Natural Heritage site, it has attracted mountaineers since the middle of the nineteenth century. The first hut was built here on a rock shelf a few feet above the ice in 1872, and it has been periodically enlarged and rebuilt ever since to cater for growing demand. Nowadays it accommodates up to a hundred people a night, especially during April and May when it is a popular base for ski-mountaineers, and the term 'hut' is something of a misnomer. Materials for the original building would have been carried all the way up from the Rhône valley by porters or, conceivably, mules. Now, it is reprovisioned on a weekly basis by helicopter, and for the hut guardian and his family it is only a thirty-minute ride on a skidoo uphill to the Jungfraujoch where the railway from Grindelwald terminates.

However, the biggest change has been to the glacier. There is nothing new about glacial recession, it has been going on for 150 years, but the process has accelerated recently. In the case of the Aletsch, the glacier has not actually retreated very much, but its surface has dropped dramatically as its volume shrinks. Konkordia in the summer becomes by midday a swamp of rotten snow cut by rushing melt-water streams. Where once climbers could walk on to the ice, there is now a metal staircase zigzagging at least a hundred metres up a vertical rock-face. At the end of a long day, it comes as a sting in the tail, especially at 2,800 metres above sea level. Every few years, as the glacier level falls, the Swiss Alpine Club is obliged to fit a new section of staircase. In the thirty years since I first visited the hut, the ice has dropped as much as it did in the previous hundred. This is not my imagination. At bends in the staircase small signs indicate the year in which this was the surface of the ice. About ten years ago I counted the number of steps out of curiosity. There were 360. Two years ago I counted again. This time, there were 450, including a ladder lashed to the bottom. It is a graphic illustration of the effect of global warming on the landscape, but it is far from unique. The same story is being repeated all over the Alps, indeed all over the world. Many small glaciers have disappeared completely; others have become no more than snow patches. Elsewhere, what used to be a smooth surface of snow has become a ridge and furrow of ice covered with rock debris. Access to and from larger glaciers becomes increasingly problematic, with treacherously loose moraine walls or ice-polished slabs to negotiate.

For most people in the west, climate change is not urgently present in their lives. It is still something to be read about in the papers, something that will affect other people, at some time in the future. But for mountaineers, one would have thought, the reality of global warming cannot be denied. The evidence is before our eyes every time we set foot on a glacier. Yet many, if not most, do appear to be in denial. The adventure travel industry is booming. The number of climbers and hikers jetting off to Greenland, Antarctica, South America and the Himalaya on a regular basis shows no sign of diminishing. Easyjet and Ryanair continue to post handsome profits. The heli-ski industry flourishes. Weekend jaunts to the Alps for both skiing and climbing are very much in vogue. Climate change? What climate change?

Satish Kumar, a former monk and editor of *Resurgence* magazine, who once walked from India to Washington via Moscow, Paris and London on a pilgrimage for peace with no money and nothing but the clothes he stood up in, believes that, in relation to planet Earth, we are all either tourists or pilgrims. We regard the Earth either as a resource available for our gratification or as a miracle of beauty and complexity to be marvelled at, valued and protected. One would expect mountaineers to be pilgrims. Mountains have been, and still are sacred in many cultures. Traditionally, even in the west, they have been sources of inspiration, symbols of aspiration and metaphors for personal quest. The early alpine climbers were, for the most part, pilgrims, entranced by what they saw and found, revelling in the discomfort and effort required. They were mountain travellers, excited by crossing a col into a different valley as much as by reaching a summit. Significant numbers were clergymen and academics seeking validation of a faith undermined by Darwin. Today, the notion of mountains as natural cathedrals, proposed by Ruskin, is deeply unfashionable. Respect, reverence even, has been replaced by a view of mountains as commodities to be marketed for the benefit of local communities and as trophies to be collected by visitors. It is an attitude to be found at all ends of the mountain spectrum from Everest to Snowdon. In the Alps it has resulted in rack railways, cable cars and chair lifts to make life easier for skiers in winter and climbers and walkers in summer, in fixed ropes to make climbs of the Matterhorn, the Eiger and countless other peaks more accessible and, most recently, in the metal clutter of *via ferrata* that have sprouted on the cliffs behind every alpine village, it seems, to provide thrills without the need for skills.

There is a paradox at the root of mountaineering that was expressed succinctly many years ago by a French alpinist, Jacques Lagarde, and quoted by Lindsay Griffin in his introduction to an Alpine Club guidebook:

> 'Ever since man has been drawn to the mountains by a love of wild nature, rigour, solitude and the unknown, all of which he found in that final refuge, he has done everything to eliminate precisely what he sought.'

Today, comfort and convenience, those twin pillars of consumerism, have prevailed in the mountains as they have everywhere else. Duvets, hot showers, beer on tap and freshly-baked bread are becoming the norm in huts, diminishing the delicious contrast and sense of appreciation that return to the valley used to bring. Bolts, GPS, radios and mobile phones have removed much of the uncertainty – and with it the adventure – of alpine climbing and ski-mountaineering. Digital cameras, Blackberries, iPhones, heart-rate monitors, and altimeter wristwatches to record every conceivable aspect of progress, all ensure that the modern mountaineer, festooned with electronic equipment, is only fleetingly, if ever, truly in the present. And if all this displacement activity should prove insufficient, we can always plug in to an iPod to avoid hearing what the mountains have to say to us. There is little time or space for that, 'sense of joy, awe and wonder' of which Satish Kumar speaks and which has been described so feelingly over the years by mountaineers as diverse as John Muir, Eric Shipton, W.H. Murray, Arne Naess and Jim Perrin.

However, it is easy enough to venture off the tourist's beaten track. We have but to leave the gizmos behind to emerge from a cocoon and be at once more acutely aware of our surroundings, more in tune with the mountain world and, as a result, probably safer also. To visit the Alps out of season when the huts are closed apart from a 'winter room' (more than half the year in fact) is to quickly rediscover 'wild nature, rigour, solitude and the unknown'. I would not wish to deny that there is value and enjoyment in the exercising of skill, judgement and experience to overcome difficulties and achieve a goal, be it a summit or a journey, or that there are plenty of occasions in the Alps when weather or snow conditions dictate that speed is of the essence. But to travel sometimes in a spirit of quietude rather than bent on accomplishment, as explorers rather than conquistadors, is to allow mountaineering to become less a matter of success or failure, and more an opportunity to notice, to observe and to be absorbed into a marvellous world. We might then come to feel more readily a part of the mountains ourselves and to feel wounded by what has been done to them and what is happening to them. We might even find it in our hearts to comprehend the plight not just of glaciers but of the whole planet and of those millions, if not billions, less fortunate than ourselves.

These sentiments may resonate with some members of the Alpine Club. Others will ridicule them as the ranting of a hair-shirt killjoy. Yet, ultimately, we are talking not about how we choose to spend our holidays but about social justice, as well as conservation in its widest sense. Over the last few years, through a mixture of concern, self-interest and coercion, most of us have made changes to the way we live our everyday lives. We recycle our paper, glass, tin and plastic. We are learning to turn off lights, televisions and computers when not in use. We see the sense of insulating our lofts and excluding draughts from windows and doors. We share transport when we can. Nobody is perfect but most of us are trying. Mountaineering, however, seems to be a compartment of our lives exempt from wider concerns. The mountaineering community needs to accept that its activities do impinge seriously on others and that changes in behaviour and lifestyle do make a difference, even if only by adding momentum to a very slowly rolling snowball. We need to ask questions about how we travel and how frequently, about how and where our clothing and equipment are made, and from what materials, and how often do they really need to be replaced. We need to make choices based on human and environmental cost rather than on pounds or dollars. Perhaps a start would be some form of carbon rationing, which would have to be self-imposed as government has shied away from the idea since the recession. An approach of 'less is more' to all aspects of our travelling and climbing could actually be enriching, enabling us to rediscover a simplicity and authenticity that used to be at the core of mountaineering. We could even find ourselves on the pilgrim path again which, returning to Satish Kumar, 'is to be on a path of adventure, to move out of our comfort zones, to let go of our prejudices and pre-conditioning, to make strides towards the unknown'.

Ilyushin transport plane on the ice runway at Patriot Hills.

26

Soaring with Icarus

I suppose I have always been a traveller. I don't remember much about it but my third birthday was celebrated on the *Warwick Castle*, of the Union Castle line, during a three-week voyage from Southampton to Mombasa. My father was a teacher in the colonial service working at schools in Kenya, Tanzania and, briefly, Egypt. Over the next eleven years that journey became almost routine for our family, varied only by the need to go round the Cape of Good Hope for a while after the Suez crisis and, on one occasion, to Trieste and across Europe by train. Flying only entered the equation when we were evacuated from Suez at twelve-hours notice, losing everything except what we could carry as hand baggage. We flew from Egypt to Malta in a flying boat and my chief recollection is of being violently sick into a paper bag.

In East Africa there were overnight train journeys from Nairobi to

Mombasa and from Dodoma to Dar-es-Salaam, but otherwise travel meant long, hot, dusty car journeys on corrugated dirt roads through the seemingly endless African bush, bare legs sticking sweatily to plastic seats, or the occasional epic mud bath during the rains. Later, as a student, my first two climbing expeditions to the Himalaya in the late sixties both required a gruelling, if culturally fascinating, overland drive through Eastern Europe, Turkey, Iran and Afghanistan to reach Pakistan. A few years on, after travelling around India by bus and train, my wife Netti and I came home overland by public transport, which was unforgettable if even more arduous. Working for the British Antarctic Survey in the early seventies involved three months on the RRS *Bransfield* on her maiden voyage making a leisurely progression south before being dropped off for a year 'on the ice'. Travel took time.

It was not until 1973 that a climbing trip to India seemed a feasible proposition by air. Prices had come down and the weight restriction was somehow evaded by buying most of our food locally and wearing big boots and duvet jackets, pockets stuffed with karabiners and pitons, on to the plane. Air travel rapidly became the norm for expeditions to the greater ranges, but travelling to the Alps remained, for me at any rate, a matter of sharing costs in a car or an uncomfortable coach journey – until the Easyjet revolution of the nineties. Suddenly, a flight to Geneva was not only ridiculously cheap but skis and climbing gear were carried free and flights could be changed for only a small penalty fee. Looking back, it is hard to realise that it is only in the last twenty years or so that we have come to take cut-price air travel so much for granted. Before that, it was definitely an expensive luxury.

All at once, many of the tensions created by enjoying my job as an alpine guide and yet valuing and often missing wife, family and home, were eased. I could come home more often and Netti could more easily join me for a week or two. For a few years I was making up to six flights to the Alps in a year as well as at least one, sometimes two or even three long-haul flights to more distant destinations. Unfortunately, this satisfactory state of affairs did not last – not for me, anyway.

Over the last ten years it has become increasingly apparent to everyone except George W. Bush and his cronies in the oil industry, that global warming is a reality. It has also become clear that of all the elements of our profligate western lifestyle that contribute to global warming, air travel is the least defensible. Flying had undoubtedly enhanced my quality of life and, indeed, made my job possible. But it was having the opposite effect on other people, especially in the poorest parts of the world, and sooner or later was going to rebound on us in the affluent west as well. I continued to fly but felt increasingly uneasy about it and limited myself to one long-haul flight a year. I began to investigate trains to the Alps but found that staggering across London and Paris with a huge rucksack and a pair of skis was just too much. After over-staying my welcome with friends in France, eventually I found a hotel in Switzerland with an all but empty nuclear bunker where I could store skis, boots, climbing gear and all the other kit needed for working in the mountains for weeks at a time. Freed up to travel relatively light, I took to commuting to the Alps by train. It proved easier than I had expected and not prohibitively expensive, either. By booking well in advance it is possible to travel from North Wales to the Rhône Valley in Switzerland for not much more than £200. While this does not compare with a fifty pence flight with Ryanair, it does not break the bank either. The journey time from door to door is about fourteen hours, only three or four hours longer than if I flew from Liverpool. After an initial hiccup when I found myself in the suburbs of Paris with twenty minutes to go, I discovered that using the Metro to travel from the Gare du Nord to the Gare du Lyon is not difficult. In fact, it is far quicker as well as far cheaper than taking a taxi.

So far, so good. At least I was doing something towards reducing my carbon footprint. But what about long-haul flights? Was I prepared to give up opportunities to work in the Himalaya or the Andes, Canada or Kenya? 'Could I call myself an international mountain guide if I never travelled outside Europe?' someone asked. And what about my desire for personal adventures and wilderness journeys? Was I ready to give up visiting the sort of genuinely remote, wild places that have been the setting for many of the most memorable experiences of my life? My concerns did not seem to resonate much either with colleagues or clients, even though every conversation seemed to lead, sooner or later, to climate change. Responses varied from 'the world is doomed. We might as well live for the day' to, 'It's up to the government to take a lead. Nothing I can do will make any difference' to, 'What's the point of Britain acting when the US refuses to budge and China and India are industrialising as fast and as cheaply as they can?' I was disappointed to find Sir Chris Bonington, an influential role model for lovers of the great outdoors, simply side-stepping the issue when confronted with it in a magazine interview. His year is arranged around regular visits to Australia to visit family, India or Nepal for mountaineering and Morocco to rock climb, as well as innumerable overseas lecture engagements and other climbing holidays, and he has no intention of giving up any of them.

In the end, I compromised. I decided to forego guiding outside Europe, albeit persuading myself that since Turkey had applied for membership of the European Union it must be in Europe. But I kept the door open for the occasional personal trip. My stance when questioned was that China and India will most certainly not move until they see Western governments taking global warming seriously. Those governments, including our own, will make token gestures like subsidising wind farms but do nothing really effective until they see that there is an electoral advantage in it. In a democracy no government will ever disturb the status quo until enough concerned citizens, aroused by journalism – responsible or otherwise – want it to. In other words, it is up to us as individuals to change our lifestyles before we can expect anything to happen.

When I flew to Vancouver in May 2007 I had not made a long-haul flight for three years and I relished the west coast wilderness, both on ski and in a sea kayak, all the more for a period of abstinence. In the wider scheme of things, attitudes towards air travel seemed to be changing, if very slowly. *Lonely Planet* came out with a new slogan 'Fly less, stay longer' which seemed an admirable sentiment, and Eurostar trains were always packed. On the other hand, *Climber* magazine saw no harm in a series of articles on weekend alpinism and skiing magazines continued to promote heli-skiing ad nauseum. On a personal level, however, it seemed to be working out. I had dramatically reduced my air miles yet I could still earn my living as a guide in the Alps and from time to time venture further afield without feeling too guilty.

Then I was offered work in Antarctica and all too easily my resolve weakened. It was thirty-five years since I had spent an extraordinary and now unrepeatable year with a dog-team on the Antarctic Peninsula. In the intervening years there had been a number of possible guiding assignments to Mount Vinson but none had come to fruition and I had come to accept that I would not be returning to the frozen continent. Now, faced with temptation, all my good intentions dissolved. Throwing ethical qualms to the winds, I accepted and took the long series of flights from London to Madrid, to Santiago, down the length of Chile to Punta Arenas and eventually across Drake's Passage and down the Antarctic Peninsula to Patriot Hills on the edge of the Ellsworth Mountains. At eighty degrees it was the furthest south I have ever been. Early in November it was still distinctly chilly with some fierce winds to boot, giving a wind-chill temperature in the minus-sixties at times, yet the sun was well above the horizon at midnight. Although my job was low-key and we made only one short journey away from the base, I loved the clarity of the light, the sense of almost infinite emptiness stretching away and the endless subtleties of colour, texture and shape to be found in a wind-blasted landscape of blue ice and sastrugi. The camaraderie of life on the base took me back to my time with BAS (British Antarctic Survey) and I was impressed by the rigorous environmental policy insisted on by ALE (Antarctic Logistics and Expeditions) to minimise pollution. I was glad to be there – until our departure was delayed by high winds and I found myself reading George Monbiot's *Heat*, a Penguin paperback I had picked up at Euston station.

Monbiot's book is not light reading. It is too detailed and painstakingly researched for that. But it is compelling, nonetheless, and convincing. His basic thesis is that the UK government's self-imposed target of reducing carbon emissions by fifty per cent by 2030 is not nearly enough to keep the level of global warming below the critical two-degree threshold; nor is there the faintest chance of even that being achieved as government policies stand at present. He believes our emissions need to be cut by no less than ninety per cent if we are to avoid global catastrophe. The good news is that he also believes, and endeavours to demonstrate, that this is, in fact, achievable, if the political will is there. However, that will is dependent entirely on us, on pressure from the electorate. Only when enough people begin to really change their habits and lifestyles and show that they mean business will the government step in with the legislation to make meaningful change possible on a wider scale – by introducing a carbon rationing system, for instance, by tightening up on building regulations, by radically changing the structure of public transport and by reversing current plans to build four thousand kilometres of new roads and to double the capacity of our airports by 2030. It is actually an optimistic book if, and only if, enough individuals are prepared to change the way they live and set the ball rolling. On the other hand, as Monbiot posits, 'If the biosphere is wrecked it will be done by nice, well-meaning, cosmopolitan people who accept the case for cutting emissions, but who won't change by one iota the way they live.'

Surprisingly, and encouragingly, Monbiot's ninety per cent reduction in carbon can be achieved in most aspects of our lives and most areas of the economy by the creative use of existing materials, techniques and technology. Only when it comes to travel are we going to have to accept drastic change. There is simply no alternative to using our cars less and regarding air travel as, at best, an occasional luxury. 'We might buy eco-friendly washing-up liquid and washable nappies, but we cancel out any carbon savings we might have made ten thousand-fold whenever we step into an aeroplane.' If we do not change the way in which we travel, hundreds of millions will be facing starvation, drought or drowning within our life-times – millions are already – our grandchildren will curse us for our folly, and the future not just of the human species but most other species also will be in jeopardy. Monbiot does not pull his punches. But nor do you get the impression that he is exaggerating or scare-mongering. He never relies on a single source or a single set of statistics, usually opts for the more optimistic figures, yet inexorably builds up his case to present us with an irrefutable, if unpalatable truth – we must stop flying: 'It means the end of shopping trips to New York, parties in Ibiza, second homes in Tuscany and, most painfully for me, political meetings in Porto Alegre – unless you believe that these activities are worth the sacrifice of the biosphere and the lives of the poor.' It also means the end of autumn sport climbing in Sardinia, Mallorca or Greece, winter sports in Canada or the US, trekking holidays in Patagonia or the Himalaya, and expeditions to Greenland or the Antarctic. Monbiot concludes his chapter on air travel with the words, 'Long distance travel, high speed and the curtailment of climate change are not compatible. If you fly, you destroy other people's lives.'

Lying in my sleeping bag 10,000 miles away from home, I read that sentence and could only cringe. My absurdly brief visit to Antarctica was clearly nothing but a selfish extravagance I had no right to indulge. It was not as if I was blissfully unaware of the issues: I simply chose to ignore them. I shall not be wearing a hair shirt as penance but I shall definitely not be returning to Antarctica. And if I was never to fly again, would it really be such a hardship? We can reach anywhere in Europe by boat, train or bus and we live in a marvellously varied and still beautiful country that I, for one, have yet to properly explore. As I write, Al Gore, speaking in Bali, has been describing climate change as 'a challenge to our moral imagination.' As out-door people we are used to accepting a challenge. Will we accept this one?

The Dix hut near Arolla being resupplied by helicopter.

27

More Adventure, Less Impact

The title of a recent Ski Symposium was 'More Adventure, Less Impact'. This seemed to be implying that most of our ski touring is not very adventurous, and that our activities are having a negative impact on the environment. I cannot disagree with either proposition. There is not much adventure involved in an average day on the Haute Route in April – a hundred people or more skinning in a deep trench from one over-crowded hut to another, skiing in effect on a piste which becomes a mogul-field on anything steep. Challenge there may be in terms of difficult skiing or unfamiliar mountaineering techniques or long, physically demanding days; there will be fantastic scenery, and beauty in the detail of the landscape; there may be the camaraderie that develops within a well-functioning group. All these things can add up to an enjoyable and rewarding tour, be it a day or a week. But they do not constitute an adventure, and adventure is what takes any outdoor experience on to a totally different plane. As for impact – you would have to be a shareholder in Exxon to deny that oil is a finite resource, and that 'peak oil' is not far away or may even have been reached, if such desperate measures as fracking and tar-sands processing are anything to go by. With its dependence on lifts and tows, piste-bashers and skidoos, snow cannon and floodlights, not to mention the whole infrastructure of mountain hotels, restaurants and apartments, the ski industry can hardly be described as environmentally friendly. Skiing is a marvellous sport in many ways, but let's be under no illusions, it's right up there with things like Formula One in terms of sustainability. Nor can ski tourers afford to feel smug, for we use lifts too and stay in huts that require regular servicing by helicopter. Clearly, there is plenty of scope both for having less impact and for being more adventurous.

There is a wonderful chapter in Primo Levi's *The Periodic Table* about his friend Sandro's propensity for 'tasting bear meat' in the mountains, which is a reminder that adventures, while memorable, are rarely enjoyable at the time. They are much more likely to be exhausting, uncomfortable, both physically and emotionally, and probably frightening, too. But they are also the occasions that will live with us when the day of perfect powder under a blue sky on the Grands Montets has long since merged with a dozen similar days. As Carl Tobin, an American climber I once nibbled bear meat with, said of an appalling bivouac somewhere, 'you don't have to be having fun to have fun.'

Admittedly, not many of us would really want, or be able to cope with, a full-on adventure every time we go into the mountains. There is, in fact, an adventure spectrum which runs from a full-blown epic, involving substantial amounts of bear meat at one end, to 'a bit of an adventure' at the other end, where there may be no more than a whiff of bear in the air. At the epic end, one is getting close to misadventure with the accompanying injuries or death. At the 'whiff of bear' end, the danger is likely to be more apparent than real, but a big effort and maybe some suffering will be required all the same, and afterwards the world is going to seem a more vivid, vibrant, amazing place because of it.

Yet 'adventure', like 'wilderness' and 'wild', has been debased as a term. It has been purloined by the marketing industry and has become a mindless slogan used to sell the tamest of treks, the most packaged of holidays. To my mind it is overused, misused and downright abused most of the time. I turned to my dictionary for a definition and, slightly to my surprise, found it to be helpful and succinct. An adventure can be, 'a risky under-taking of uncertain outcome' or it can be, 'an exciting or unexpected event or course of events'. The key words relevant to us are risk, uncertainty, excitement and unexpected. Well, an element of risk is inherent in the mountain environment, as is the possibility of the unexpected occurring, be it an avalanche blocking a road or a crevasse opening up under our feet. Excitement too is to be found readily enough in our skiing or climbing. That leaves only the element of uncertainty standing in the way of every ski tour being an adventure. And it's certainly true that we do everything we can to reduce that uncertainty, whether it's using GPS to keep tabs on our position or poring over guidebooks and studying internet pictures. But the main factor that militates against uncertainty is simply the sheer number of people around in the mountains these days. I think as a pre-requisite for adventure in the outdoors one has to add 'Few, if any, other people in the vicinity'.

Given the overcrowding typical of the Alps, how then can we find more adventure? The obvious solution, reflected in the pages of every magazine and journal you look at, is to find ever wilder and more remote corners of the globe to go skiing and ski touring. Over Christmas, an Eagle Ski Club party will be in Antarctica. Last year the club expedition was to South America. Next year Greenland and Alaska have been proposed, and trips to India, Kyrgyzstan, British Columbia and the US are two a penny. But this trend brings one hard up against 'less impact' and the need to fly to all these exciting destinations.

In other words, climate change. A lot of people I come across do not believe that the planet is really warming up, or else they believe that it is entirely due to natural causes rather than the interference of mankind. A very convenient belief if you happen to be a skier! According to the *New Scientist* this attitude is becoming more rather than less prevalent, to the point where most Republican candidates for the last presidential election publicly disputed global warming. An editorial commented, 'When candidates for the highest office in the land appear to spurn reason, embrace anecdote over scientific evidence, and even portray scientists as the perpetrators of a massive hoax, there is reason to worry.'

Given that every proper scientist I know is convinced of the reality of climate change, it has long puzzled me why so many people doubt it. Last summer I found out. Working in the Alps for several weeks and attempting to keep up with the news at a time of financial turmoil (when the Swiss franc, the euro and the pound almost achieved parity), I found myself reading a wider than normal cross section of English language newspapers. I discovered that the editorial policy of each of the three most widely available – *The Times*, *The Telegraph* and the *Daily Mail* – was to rubbish the whole idea of climate change and to generally muddy the waters of the debate. Presumably this reflects the short-term commercial interests of their billionaire owners, though it must also be in the cynical knowledge that readers will buy a paper that tells them what they want to hear.

By contrast, Chris Goodall in *How to Lead a Low Carbon Life* is unequivocal that, 'Travelling by air, in contrast to the train, is an almost unmitigated disaster for the environment.' Unfortunately, most skiers and climbers have developed, in just a few short years, a flying habit that threatens to become an addiction that will be very hard to break.

I'm not going to suggest that we all give up flying completely. But I do suggest that as individuals we revive the old-fashioned notion of restraint. As Aristotle said, the key to happiness is 'moderation in all things'. Our attitude to flying is rapidly becoming immoderate. Perhaps we can consciously try to reduce our carbon emissions by avoiding flights within the UK or long weekends in the Alps. Perhaps we can ski for a single three-week block, rather than three separate one-week holidays, which has other advantages in terms of fitness and acclimatisation. Perhaps inveterate expeditioners could ration themselves to one long haul flight every other year instead of two a year? Perhaps more of us could investigate how to obtain cheap train fares? (I've heard one skier, on a six-figure salary, complain that the train costs too much) or look at the even cheaper bus option.

So, coming back to adventure, perhaps we should be looking for it not at the ends of the earth, but within Europe or around the Mediterranean in places like Turkey, the Lebanon, Corsica, where the maps tend to be sketchy and the mountains empty. There have been some very adventurous tours in recent years to places like Albania, Romania, the Tatra, Slovenia, Crete – the list goes on. Then there is that huge, empty magnificent mountain country Norway (and Sweden too come to that).

But alas, they too all tend to involve flying considerable distances (what a tragedy it was when the ferry to Bergen shut). So, rather than promoting these undeniably attractive destinations, I would like to take a closer look at how we can find more adventure nearer home, in the Alps.

- An obvious starting point is simply to go to an area new to you, which I suspect most people tend to do, anyway. But, once there, don't rely too heavily on the guidebook. Use it to glean basic information about huts, access, crossable cols and so on, but then avoid recommended routes. Put simply, if you follow the guidebook you will be in a trench. Make up your own and there's a good chance you'll be on your own. Adventure lies the way 'less travelled'.
- Leave the electronic gadgets at home. If you carry them, you will use them. Using GPS for navigation and an iPhone to obtain daily updates of avalanche and weather bulletins gives you peace of mind and reduces stress and uncertainty. But stress and uncertainty are precisely what adventure is about. All these gizmos are doing for ski touring what bolts have done for rock climbing – you accomplish more but it means less.
- If you are quite experienced, try going for day tours on your own. If you can find terrain with no old tracks, it can feel quite adventurous. With no one to talk to, you notice a whole lot more. And with no one to watch, you don't have to worry about how many tight little turns you make, and can concentrate on finding a safe flowing line down the mountain.
- Use unguarded huts or bivvy shelters. This means carrying more weight and sometimes being a bit chilly, but the plus side is there is unlikely to be anyone else there and you have the advantage of eating when you feel like it and getting up in the morning when you want to rather than when it suits the guardian. Admittedly, I've had a few epics in Italy involving bivvy huts that have been given a makeover so they look very smart, but absolutely everything has been removed in the way of pots and pans, cutlery and crockery. It's amazing what you can improvise when you have to!
- Go out of season, when most huts will be shut anyway, which usually means January, February or early March now that huts are opening earlier. In quite a few places huts still don't open until Easter. In Switzerland, especially, unguarded huts can be very snug.

Or don't even use huts. With modern lightweight tents, the weight need not be prohibitive. One of the most enterprising ski trips I know of was Ian Johnson and a friend skiing the Haute Route one January, tenting or snow-holing the whole way. Now that's what I call an adventure!